Compensation for Environmental Damage Under International Law

Inspired by recent litigation, this book identifies and critically appraises the manifold and varied approaches to calculating compensation for damage caused to the environment.

It examines a wide range of practice on compensation – in general and specifically for environmental damage – from that of international courts and tribunals, as well as international commissions and regimes, to municipal approaches and other disciplines such as economics and philosophy. *Compensation for Environmental Damage Under International Law* synthesises these approaches with a view to identifying their blind spots, bringing clarity to an area where there exists broad discrepancy, and charting best practices that appropriately balance the manifold interests at stake. In particular, it is argued that best practice methodologies should ensure compensation serves to fully repair the environment, reflect the emerging ecosystems approach and any implications environmental damage may have for climate change, as well as take into account relevant equitable considerations.

This book is essential reading for academics, practitioners and students working in the field of environmental law.

Dr Jason Rudall is Assistant Professor of Public International Law at Leiden University in The Netherlands.

Routledge Research in International Environmental Law

Environmental Governance in Europe and Asia
A Comparative Study of Institutional and Legislative Frameworks
Jona Razzaque

Climate Change, Forests and REDD
Lessons for Institutional Design
Edited by Joyeeta Gupta, Nicolien van der Grijp and Onno Kuik

International Environmental Law and the Conservation of Coral Reefs
Edward J. Goodwin

International Environmental Law and the International Court of Justice
Aleksandra Cavoski

Enforcement of International Environmental Law
Challenges and Responses at the International Level
Martin Hedemann-Robinson

Marine Pollution, Shipping Waste and International Law
Gabriela Argüello

Compensation for Environmental Damage Under International Law
Jason Rudall

For more information about this series, please visit: www.routledge.com/ Routledge-Research-in-International-Environmental-Law/book-series/ INTENVLAW

Compensation for Environmental Damage Under International Law

Jason Rudall

Routledge
Taylor & Francis Group

LONDON AND NEW YORK

First published 2020
by Routledge
2 Park Square, Milton Park, Abingdon, Oxon OX14 4RN

and by Routledge
605 Third Avenue, New York, NY 10017

First issued in paperback 2021

Routledge is an imprint of the Taylor & Francis Group, an informa business

British Library Cataloguing-in-Publication Data
A catalogue record for this book is available from the British Library

Library of Congress Cataloging-in-Publication Data
Names: Rudall, Jason, author.
Title: Compensation for environmental damage under international law /
    Jason Rudall.
Description: Abingdon, Oxon ; New York, NY : Routledge, 2020. | Series:
    Routledge research in international law | Includes bibliographical
    references and index.
Identifiers: LCCN 2019056567 (print) | LCCN 2019056568 (ebook) |
    ISBN 9780367353230 (hardback) | ISBN 9780429341496 (ebook)
Subjects: LCSH: Liability for environmental damages. | Government
    liability (International law) | Environmental law, International.
Classification: LCC K955 .R838 2020 (print) | LCC K955 (ebook) | DDC
    344.04/6—dc23
LC record available at https://lccn.loc.gov/2019056567
LC ebook record available at https://lccn.loc.gov/2019056568

ISBN 13: 978-1-03-223879-1 (pbk)
ISBN 13: 978-0-367-35323-0 (hbk)

Typeset in Times New Roman
by Apex CoVantage, LLC

Contents

Introduction

Until recently there had been scant precedent among international courts and tribunals for valuing environmental damage. However, over the last few years several cases reveal that international courts and tribunals are now willing to award States pecuniary relief for harm caused to their natural environment.[1] This book critically appraises the valuation methodologies adopted in these cases. It does so in light of the wide range of methods available, including in the practice of other international institutions like the United Nations Compensation Commission and treaty regimes, those that feature in domestic legal systems and alternatives proposed by economists and philosophers.

The issues at stake in awarding compensation for environmental damage

The February 2018 decision of the International Court of Justice (ICJ) in *Certain Activities Carried out by Nicaragua in the Border Area (Costa Rica v. Nicaragua) – Compensation* is the first time that the ICJ has awarded compensation for environmental damage. In fact, the ICJ has only ever made three compensation awards.[2] Despite this, the ICJ boldly asserted in this case that 'damage to the environment, and the consequent impairment or loss of the ability of the environment to provide goods and services, is compensable under international law'.[3] The significance of this judgment should not be underestimated. Indeed, it will likely serve as a touchstone for future courts and tribunals in cases involving environmental compensation. That said, there are many aspects of the ICJ's methodology and reasoning in this case that are unsatisfactory.[4]

The emerging practice of international courts and tribunals awarding environmental compensation is also evident in several investor–State disputes. In *Burlington Resources Inc. v. Ecuador*, for example, a tribunal constituted under the International Centre for the Settlement of Investment

Disputes (ICSID) ordered the payment of USD41 million in compensation for environmental damage caused by the claimant.[5] It did so on the basis of Ecuadorian national law but the methodology adopted by the Tribunal merits consideration. In *Perenco v. Ecuador*, having reviewed all of the evidence put forward by the parties and a tribunal-appointed expert, another ICSID tribunal was of the view in an interim decision that Perenco would likely be liable for causing environmental damage in Ecuador.[6]

As will become evident from a consideration of these cases in this book, there are many ways of calculating monetary compensation for environmental damage, and their outcomes vary significantly. This is particularly apparent in the major discrepancies that often exist between claimant, respondent and tribunal assessments of environmental damage. For example, in the ICJ case, Costa Rica claimed for almost USD7 million in damages, while Nicaragua estimated that Costa Rica was not entitled to anything more than around USD190,000. The Court ultimately awarded almost USD380,000, which represented about 5% of Costa Rica's claim. In light of the vast sums at stake and the wildly different calculations, it is appropriate that coherent guidance on assessing environmental damage in monetary terms is developed.

A further aspect of the emerging practice on environmental compensation is the extent to which the assessments made by international courts and tribunals reflect a full picture of the environmental damage. In these recent international cases, judges and arbitrators have largely relied on what economists call use-values, market prices and restoration costs.[7] As such, the values of resources have been calculated by reference to techniques such as replacement cost, contingent valuation or benefit transfer approaches, among others. These methods can have significant blind spots and often fail to account for environmental damage in its entirety, such as a diminution in carbon sequestration that can contribute to climate change, for example.

One way to ameliorate these shortcomings would be to incorporate an eco-system services approach, a greater appreciation for non-use values and the intrinsic value of the environment, as well as equitable considerations that could take account of any climate change dimension and the behaviour of the parties in the calculation of environmental compensation. While such calculations are undoubtedly more complex, they are not impossible, and international institutions as well as scholars have suggested potential frameworks.[8]

Methodologies that encompass broader notions of damage will certainly be more appropriate for calculating compensation for harm caused by climate change. Given the growing wave of national and regional climate litigation,[9] it is only a matter of time before an international tribunal has to adjudicate a case of this kind involving environmental compensation. This is an important reason for clarifying the current practice.

Whether the conduct of the parties in a given case should be accounted for in assessments of compensation is another important aspect to clarify. While many agree that it is not possible to award punitive damages under international law, others suggest it should be appropriate to factor in elements such as gravely wrongful conduct, the degree of fault, intention, bad faith and negligence in the calculation of compensation. Similarly, certain courts and tribunals have confirmed that punitive compensation is not permitted under international law,[10] while other international tribunals have nevertheless awarded relief that reflects the egregious behaviour of a party.[11] Dissenting ICJ judges in the *Costa Rica v. Nicaragua* case suggested the gravity of Nicaragua's wrongful behaviour should have been taken into account in the assessment of damages.[12] Moreover, the International Law Commission (ILC) and the *Institut de droit international* have both indicated that the behaviour of the parties is relevant to the evaluation of compensation, as are considerations of equity.[13]

The study will also consider several related questions that are relevant to the assessment of environmental damage and the valuation of compensation thereto. This includes, for example, the role that experts could play in the calculation of environmental compensation, especially in light of their increasing prominence in international courts and tribunals.

While not directly concerned with environmental compensation, several other cases are nevertheless apposite to this developing area of law. One example is the Inter-American Court of Human Rights' recently issued Advisory Opinion on *The Environment and Human Rights*.[14] Confirming the link between the realisation of human rights and the existence of a healthy environment, the Court found that States should take measures to ensure significant environmental harm is not caused to individuals within or beyond their territory.[15] In establishing a justiciable right to a healthy environment under the American Convention on Human Rights, this Opinion may well open the door for individual litigants to bring a case where this right has been interfered with, even extraterritorially. This is, once again, especially relevant in the context of growing climate litigation. Similarly, the Human Rights Committee has affirmed a duty to protect individuals from damage to the environment under the International Covenant on Civil and Political Rights.[16] In this context, the nexus between human rights and environmental change has become increasingly evident. The impact that this may have on the assessment of damages will also be considered in the book.

Developing notions of environmental damage

Alongside a consideration of compensation approaches, it will be instructive to consider understandings of environmental damage. It has been said that '[g]eneral international law neither defines environmental damage nor provides any guidance as to how it should be valued. Without the study of State practice, and of national law, that position is unlikely to change'.[17] Some guidance can be derived from various international conventional and judicial sources, and an emerging ecosystems approach in definitions of environmental damage and pollution is evident.[18] A more complex understanding of the environment, by adopting an ecosystem services approach, can help to reveal the values of the environment that would otherwise remain hidden, such as its capacity for carbon sequestration and the interdependency of ecosystem species. It is unfortunate that the ICJ did not adopt a more robust application of the ecosystem services approach in its recent decision on environmental compensation.[19] Judicial actors have often played an important role in the development of international environmental law, particularly in cases of the ICJ, and they have the potential to so in this context as well.

The judicial development of international environmental law

The basic principle of international environmental law was set out by an arbitral tribunal in the middle of the twentieth century. The *Trail Smelter* case[20] was one of the first international cases in which environmental damage was addressed. In this case, the United States accused Canada of causing environmental damage to the State of Washington through its industrial activities at a smelting plant across the border. The arbitral tribunal held Canada responsible. It was noted that a State was 'not to use or permit the use of its territory in such a manner as to cause injury by fumes in or to the territory of another or the properties or persons therein, when the case is of serious consequences and the injury is established by clear and convincing evidence'.[21] As such, this case stands for the so-called no harm principle according to which States must not cause significant transboundary harm to their neighbouring countries.

The ICJ reaffirmed this principle in the *Corfu Channel* case in 1949.[22] This was a case between the UK and Albania in which the former had its naval ships damaged and lost sailors after hitting mines in Albanian waters. Beyond international courts and tribunals, the no-harm principle was also affirmed by States under the 1972 United Nations Stockholm Declaration on the Human Environment. Subsequently, in an advisory opinion on the *Legality of the Threat or Use of Nuclear Weapons* in 1996, the ICJ said in an often-cited paragraph:

> The environment is not an abstraction but represents the living space, the quality of life and the very health of human beings, including

generations unborn. The existence of the general obligation of States to ensure that activities within their jurisdiction and control respect the environment of other States or of areas beyond national control is now part of the corpus of international law relating to the environment.[23]

A year later in 1997, Hungary and Slovakia came before the ICJ in a dispute known as the *Gabčíkovo-Nagymaros* case.[24] This concerned a dispute over a joint dam project that the two States had agreed to many years before in a treaty between them. While emphasizing the importance of the so-called *pacta sunt servanda* principle, that is the idea that agreements should be kept, the Court nevertheless emphasised that new norms on the protection of the environment should be taken into consideration in the interpretation of existing treaties between States as well as in the negotiation of new treaties.[25]

Just over a decade later, the ICJ would be faced with another significant case involving environmental protection, that between Argentina and Uruguay involving the construction of a pulp mill on the River Uruguay, which flows between the two countries. In the *Pulp Mills* case, the ICJ recognised that the conduct of environmental impact assessments prior to the commencement of projects presenting a transboundary environmental risk had become an obligation of general international law.[26]

The resort to experts in scientific matters has also been encouraged by the ICJ in some cases, particularly since the *Pulp Mills* case.[27] Moreover, in their Dissenting Opinion in that case, Judges Simma and Al-Khasawneh stressed the importance of referring to experts in cases involving complex scientific matters.[28] Following *Pulp Mills*, scientific experts were resorted to in other cases having environmental dimensions such as the *Whaling in the Antarctic* case,[29] the *Construction of a Road in Costa Rica along the San Juan River* case[30] and the *Maritime Delimitation in the Caribbean Sea and the Pacific Ocean* case.[31] Beyond cases having an environmental dimension, the ICJ has appointed its own experts to assess the compensation amount in cases involving the award of monetary damages.[32]

A roadmap for this study

This book aims to provide much needed clarity on all of these issues. As for the structure of this book, Chapter 1 considers monetary compensation in international law generally. Chapter 2 looks closely at the developing practice around compensation for environmental damage under international law in the context of international courts and tribunals. Chapter 3 assesses other international institutions and conventional frameworks that have addressed environmental compensation and developed understandings of environmental damage. It considers, for example, the practice of the UN Compensation Commission (UNCC), the International Oil Pollution Compensation (IOPC) regime and many others, as well as tracing the emerging notion of an ecosystem services approach in several international instruments. Chapter 4 provides an insight into the approaches taken in legislative frameworks and by domestic courts at the national and regional levels, with a particular focus on US and European Union (EU) practice. Chapter 5 considers the manifold techniques for assessing environmental damage and its valuation from economic and philosophical perspectives. It is hoped that this will provide lawyers with greater conceptual clarity as well as demonstrate the wide variety of techniques available, along with each of their advantages and disadvantages. The concluding chapter synthesises the findings of the study and aims to suggest avenues for development based on the best practices in protecting our environment.

Notes

1 *Certain Activities Carried Out By Nicaragua in the Border Area (Costa Rica v. Nicaragua) (Compensation)*, ICJ General List No. 150 (2 February 2018); *Burlington Resources v. Ecuador*, ICSID Case No. ARB/08/5, Decision on Ecuador's Counterclaim (7 February 2017); *Perenco v. Ecuador and Empresa Estatal Petróleos del Ecuador (Petroecuador)*, ICSID Case No. ARB/08/6, Interim Decision on the Environmental Counterclaim (11 August 2015).
2 *Corfu Channel Case (Assessment of the Amount of Compensation Due from the People's Republic of Albania to the United Kingdom of Great Britain and Northern Ireland)* [1949] ICJ Rep 244; *Case Concerning Ahmadou Sadio Diallo (Republic of Guinea v. Democratic Republic of the Congo)*, Compensation, Judgment [2012] ICJ Rep 324 and *Costa Rica v. Nicaragua (Compensation)*, op cit.
3 *Costa Rica v. Nicaragua (Compensation)*, op cit, para 42.
4 See Jason Rudall, 'Certain Activities Carried Out By Nicaragua in the Border Area (Costa Rica v. Nicaragua) – Compensation Owed by the Republic of Nicaragua to the Republic of Costa Rica' 112(2) (2018) *American Journal of International Law* 288, and infra.
5 *Burlington Resources v. Ecuador*, op cit.
6 *Perenco v. Ecuador*, op cit.
7 *Costa Rica v. Nicaragua (Compensation)*, op cit (the ICJ ultimately adopted a market price approach, assigning market values to goods and services provided by the environment); *Burlington Resources v. Ecuador*, op cit (the tribunal applied a strict liability remediation costs approach under Ecuadorian domestic law); *Perenco v. Ecuador*, op cit (the tribunal appointed its own expert to value environmental damage under Ecuadorian law).
8 Conceptual Framework Working Group of the Millennium Ecosystem Assessment, *Ecosystems and Human Well-Being: A Framework for Assessment* (Island Press, 2003); UNEP Working Group on Liability and Compensation for Environmental Damage arising from Military Activities, *Liability and Compensation for Environmental Damage* (UNEP, 1998), para 44; Michael Bowman,

'Biodiversity, Intrinsic Value, and the Definition and Valuation of Environmental Harm' in Michael Bowman and Alan Boyle (eds.), *Environmental Damage in International and Comparative Law: Problems of Definition and Valuation* (Oxford University Press, 2002); Freya Mathews, *The Ecological Self* (Routledge, 1991); Robin Attfield, *The Ethics of Environmental Concern* (2nd ed., University of Georgia Press, 1991).

9 See, for example, *The Netherlands v. Urgenda*, No. 200.178.245/01 (2018); *Juliana v. United States*, No. 6:15-cv-1517-TC (2016); *Air Transport of America et al v. Secretary of State for Energy and Climate Change* [2001] ECR II-864; *The People's Climate Case (Armando Ferrão Carvalho and Others v. European Parliament and Council*, No. T-330/18 (pending).

10 *Costa Rica v. Nicaragua (Compensation)*, Dissenting Opinion of Judge Ad Hoc Dugard, op cit, para 31.

11 See, for example, *I'm Alone Case*, III [1933–1935] Reports of International Arbitral Awards 1609; *Rainbow Warrior Affair*, XX [1990] Reports of International Arbitral Awards 215; *Eritrea-Ethiopia Claims Commission*, Final Award, 26 [2009] Reports of International Arbitral Awards 631, paras 103, 310–12.

12 *Costa Rica v. Nicaragua (Compensation)*, op cit, Dissenting Opinion of Judge Ad Hoc Dugard, paras 40–6.

13 Draft Articles on the Responsibility of States for Internationally Wrongful Acts II(2) YBILC (2001), 100; L'Institut de droit international, 'Final Report on Responsibility and Liability under International Law for Environmental Damage' (1997) Annuaire de L'Institut de droit international, 339.

14 *The Environment and Human Rights (State Obligations in Relation to the Environment in the Context of the Protection and Guarantee of the Rights to Life and to Personal Integrity: Interpretation and Scope of Articles 4(1) and 5(1) of the American Convention on Human Rights)*, Advisory Opinion OC-23/17, Inter-Am Ct HR (ser. A) No. 23.

15 Ibid.

16 *Portillo Cáceres v. Paraguay*, Communication Number 2751/2016 (CCPR/C/126/D/2751/2016), 9 August 2019.

17 Alan Boyle, 'Reparation for Environmental Damage in International Law: Some Preliminary Problems', in Bowman and Boyle (eds.), *Environmental Damage in International and Comparative Law: Problems of Definition and Valuation*, op cit, 26.

18 See Owen McIntyre, 'Protection and Preservation of Freshwater Ecosystems (Articles 20–23)' in Laurence Boisson de Chazournes, Makane Moïse Mbengue, Mara Tignino, Komlan Sangbana, and Jason Rudall (eds.), *The UN Convention on the Law of the Non-Navigational Uses of International Watercourses: A Commentary* (Oxford University Press, 2018); Jason Rudall, 'The Interplay between the UN Watercourses Convention and International Environmental Law' in Boisson de Chazournes, Mbengue, Tignino, Sangbana, and Rudall (eds.), *The UN Convention on the Law of the Non-Navigational Uses of International Watercourses: A Commentary*, op cit; see also Owen McIntyre, 'The Role of Customary Rules and Principles in the Environmental Protection of Shared International Freshwater Resources' 46(1) (2006) *Natural Resources Journal* 157. The ICJ in the *Gabčíkovo-Nagymaros* case appears to have connected the ecosystem approach with the precautionary principle:

> The Court is mindful that, in the field of environmental protection, vigilance and prevention are required on account of the often irreversible

character of damage to the environment and of the limitations inherent in the very mechanism of reparation of this type of damage.

Case Concerning the Gabčikovo-Nagymaros Project (Hungary/Slovakia) [1997] ICJ Rep 7, para 140.

19 See chapter 2 on the ICJ's apparent adoption of the so-called 'corrected analysis' of the ecosystem services approach.
20 *Trail Smelter Case (United States/Canada)* III (1938 and 1941) Reports of International Arbitral Awards 1905.
21 Ibid.
22 *Corfu Channel Case*, op cit.
23 *Legality of the Threat or Use of Nuclear Weapons* [1996] ICJ Rep 226, para 29.
24 *Case Concerning the Gabčikovo-Nagymaros Project*, op cit.
25 Ibid., para 140.
26 Ibid.
27 *Pulp Mills on the River Uruguay (Argentina v. Uruguay)* [2010] ICJ Rep 14, particularly para 167.
28 Ibid., Dissenting Opinion of Judges Simma and Al-Khasawneh, paras 3 and 8.
29 *Whaling in the Antarctic (Australia v. Japan)* [2014] ICJ Rep 226, paras 74–5.
30 *Construction of a Road in Costa Rica along the San Juan River (Nicaragua v. Costa Rica)*, Judgment (16 December 2015), paras 45, 175–6, 204.
31 *Maritime Delimitation in the Caribbean Sea and the Pacific Ocean (Costa Rica v. Nicaragua) / Land Boundary in the Northern Part of Isla Portillos (Costa Rica v. Nicaragua)*, General List Nos. 157 and 165 (2 February 2018), paras 14, 71, 73, and 86.
32 *Corfu Channel Case*, op cit; *Diallo*, op cit.

1 Compensation under international law

Introduction

Awarding compensation has had a mixed practice in international law. While the ICJ has only ever made three compensation awards,[1] pecuniary relief is common in other dispute settlement mechanisms. This chapter appraises the general principles that have governed compensation as a means of reparation. It surveys, in particular, the guidance provided by the Draft Articles on the Responsibility of States for Internationally Wrongful Acts and their commentaries and the major approaches to valuation adopted by international courts and tribunals, as well as scholarly opinion on compensation in international law. The chapter begins, however, by setting out the basic framework for reparations under international law.

Reparations under international law

Reparation is the remedy sought for damage that has been caused by the breach of an obligation. It is a fundamental principle of international law that a breach results in another obligation to repair the damage adequately, and this usually requires that an injured party should be put back in the same position as if the illegal act had not occurred.[2] Article 31(1) of the ILC Draft Articles provides that a responsible State must 'make full reparation for the injury caused'. The ILC has indicated that the formulation is intended to be 'inclusive' in this respect, covering as it does 'material and moral damage broadly understood'.[3] That said, the ILC also intended that 'merely abstract concerns or general interests of a State which is individually unaffected by the breach' do not fall within the remit.[4] Material damage is 'damage to property or other interests of the State and its nationals which is assessable in financial terms' while moral damage 'includes such items as individual pain and suffering, loss of loved ones or personal affront associated with an intrusion on one's home or private life'.[5]

Reparation may include restitution, compensation, rehabilitation, satisfaction or guarantees of non-repetition. Under the ILC's Draft Articles, restitution, compensation and satisfaction are provided for in Article 34. Restitution means re-establishing the circumstances that existed prior to the commission of the wrongful act. Article 35 of the Draft Articles notes that restitution should be preferred unless it is materially impossible or involves a disproportionate burden to the award of compensation. Compensation is monetary relief for material and non-material loss. Satisfaction may include a formal acknowledgement of fault, recognition of the wrongful nature of the act committed, an apology or prosecutions of those responsible. Rehabilitation can be the provision of certain services to help with recovery from the damage suffered, such as medical care for example. Guarantees of non-repetition are declarations that wrongful acts will cease and might entail the adoption of specific measures or institutional reform to ensure the breach does not occur again.

An obligation to repair damage in full can still be incumbent on the responsible State where there are concurrent causes of the damage, except in situations of contributory fault. This was the case in the *Corfu Channel* dispute.[6] Albania had not been responsible for laying the mines that damaged British naval ships, but it had been responsible for failing to warn the United Kingdom about them. Nevertheless, it was found liable to pay the full amount of the United Kingdom's claim.[7] A similar approach was evident in the *United States Diplomatic and Consular Staff in Tehran* case, in which Iran was responsible for failing to protect hostages seized by militant students who were not acting as organs or agents of the State.[8] This could similarly be the case where a natural event compounds damage.[9] That said, where part of the injury is severable from that caused by the responsible State, the responsible State may not be responsible for all the damage caused by its wrongful conduct. Tribunals may place the burden of proof on the responsible State to demonstrate that damage was not attributable to it.[10]

A short history of reparations

An early indication of the duty to repair the damage caused by a wrongful act is evident in the work of Francisco de Vitoria, who described in the mid-sixteenth century the obligation incumbent on an enemy who had committed a wrongful act to redress any damage they had created.[11] Hugo Grotius spoke of the duty to repair damage in *De Jure Belli ac Pacis* of 1625.[12] Similarly, Samuel Pufendorf in his 1672 *Elementorum Jurisprudentiae Universalis – Libri Duo* explained how those who caused damage as a result of a wrongful act had to 'restore as much as he contributed to the damage'.[13] Pufendorf went on to describe that the injured could not peacefully reconcile with the wrongdoer without compensation.[14] It became customary to pay war indemnities to the victors of a conflict. In the second half of the eighteenth century, Christian Wolf noted in his *Principes du droit de la nature et des gens* and *Jus Gentium Methodo Scientica Pertractatum* that any wrong caused to an individual of another State or another State at large was obliged to repair that damage.[15] In the early twentieth century, a duty to repair a wrongful act was generally considered as an obligation under customary international law.[16] The Permanent Court of International Justice (PCIJ) articulated the seminal formulation of reparation which retains significance to the present day. In its 1928 *Chorów Factory* case, the Court explained that

> It is a principle of international law that the breach of an engagement involves an obligation to make reparation in an adequate form. Reparation therefore is the indispensable complement of a failure to apply a convention and there is no necessity for this to be stated in the Convention itself. Differences relating to reparations, which may be due by reason of failure to apply a convention, are consequently differences relating to its application.[17]

And went on to observe:

> The essential principle contained in the actual notion of an illegal act – a principle which seems to be established by international practice and in particular by the decisions of arbitral tribunals – is that reparation must, as far as possible, wipe out all the consequences of the illegal act and re-establish the situation which would, in all probability, have existed if that act had not been committed. Restitution in kind, or, if this is not possible, payment of a sum corresponding to the value which a restitution in kind would bear; the award, if need be, of damages for loss sustained which would not be covered by restitution in kind or payment in place of it.[18]

The PCIJ and other international tribunals have also helped to develop the notion of compensation under international law, which we will now turn to consider.

Compensation under international law

While there is a preference for restitution under international law, compensation has been expressed in both case law and treaties as an appropriate means of reparation under international law in certain circumstances.

Compensation may be for damage actually resulting from an internationally wrongful act and indirect or remote damage is generally excluded. A principle for determining the amount of compensation was offered by the PCIJ in the *Chorzów Factory* case:

> Restitution in kind, or, if this is not possible, payment of a sum corresponding to the value which a restitution in kind would bear; the award, if need be, of damages for loss sustained which would be covered by restitution in kind or payment in place of it – such are the principles which should serve to determine the amount of compensation due for an act contrary to international law.[19]

In the 1922 case of *Norwegian Shipowner's Claims*, the Permanent Court of Arbitration noted the approach that should be taken in the assessment of compensation for damage to property and, where this was not possible, the role that equity may play in the determination:

> It is common ground between the parties that just compensation, as it is understood in the United States, should be liberally awarded, and that it should be based upon the net value of the property taken. It has been somewhat difficult to fix real market value of some of these shipbuilding contracts. That value must be assessed *ex aequo et bono*.[20]

In the *Rainbow Warrior* case of 1990, an arbitral tribunal confirmed that 'any violation by a State of any obligation, of whatever origin, gives rise to State responsibility and consequently to the duty of reparation'[21] and in the *Gabčíkovo-Nagymaros* case went on to re-affirm that 'it is a well-established rule of international law that an injured State is entitled to obtain compensation from the State which has committed an internationally wrongful act for the damage caused by it'.[22] In this case, however, the Court also indicated that it had

> not been asked at this stage to determine the quantum of damages due, but to indicate on what basis they should be paid. . . . Given the fact . . . that there have been intersecting wrongs by both Parties, the Court wishes to observe that the issue of compensation could satisfactorily be resolved in the framework of an overall settlement if each of the Parties were to renounce or cancel all financial claims and counterclaims.[23]

It nevertheless went on to find that

> unless the Parties otherwise agree, Hungary shall compensate Slovakia for the damage sustained by Czechoslovakia and by Slovakia on account of the suspension and abandonment by Hungary of works for which it

was responsible; and Slovakia shall compensate Hungary for the damage it has sustained on account of putting into operation of the 'provisional solution' by Czechoslovakia and its maintenance by Slovakia.[24]

Through its case law, the ICJ has provided for a three-step approach for determining the amount of compensation owed. These three elements include (1) that a State has suffered an injury; (2) there is a direct causal link between the unlawful act of the responsible State and the injury of the injured State; and (3) the quantum of compensation.[25]

The ICJ has also confirmed that compensation is awarded on the basis of the submissions of the parties and it has expressed a preference for separate proceedings so that it can hear evidence concerning the quantum of compensation to be awarded.[26] In the *Fisheries Jurisdiction* case, the ICJ discussed the circumstances in which it could award compensation:

> In order to award compensation the Court can only act with reference to a concrete submission as to the existence and the amount of each head of damage. Such an award must be based on precise grounds and detailed evidence concerning those acts which have been committed, taking into account all relevant facts of each incident and their consequences in the circumstances of the case. It is only after receiving evidence on these matters that the Court can satisfy itself that each concrete claim is well founded in fact and in law.[27]

In the *Military and Paramilitary Activities in and Against Nicaragua* case, the ICJ confirmed that compensation was to be based on the submissions of the parties.[28] The Court declined to make an assessment of compensation owed in this case, partly in view of the respondent party's non-appearance and partly to avoid creating any obstacles to a negotiated settlement. Similarly, in *United States Diplomatic and Consular Staff in Tehran*, the ICJ declared that the US had a right to reparations from Iran but indicated that a subsequent proceeding would be necessary to determine the type and quantum of reparations.[29] The latter never occurred. It has similarly bifurcated proceedings in *Armed Activities on the Territory of the Congo*[30] and *Certain Activities Carried out by Nicaragua in the Border Area (Costa Rica v. Nicaragua) and Construction of a Road in Costa Rica Along the San Juan River (Nicaragua v. Costa Rica)*.[31] In the *Wall* Advisory Opinion, the ICJ deemed it appropriate for Israel to pay compensation, although refrained from specifying the quantum.[32] It was of the view that

> Israel is accordingly under an obligation to return the land, orchards, olive groves and other immovable property seized from any natural or legal person for purposes of construction of the wall in the Occupied

Palestinian Territory. In the event such restitution should prove to be materially impossible, Israel has an obligation to compensate the persons in question for the damage suffered. The Court considers that Israel also has an obligation to compensate, in accordance with the applicable rules of international law, all natural or legal persons having suffered any form of material damage as a result of the wall's construction.[33]

In certain circumstances, compensation may not be awarded. The ILC has commented that the inclusion of the term 'financially assessable damage' in Article 36(2) of the Draft Articles on State Responsibility 'is intended to exclude compensation for what is sometimes referred to as "moral damage" to a State, i.e. the affront or injury caused by a violation of rights not associated with actual damage to property or persons'.[34]

There are cases where the ICJ has deemed compensation to be an inappropriate form of reparation. This was the case in *Application of the Convention on the Prevention and Punishment of the Crime of Genocide* in which the Court declined Bosnia's request for compensation.[35] Its reasoning was that there was not sufficient evidence of causation between the breach and the injury. It thus could not 'regard as proven a causal nexus between [Serbia's] violation of its obligation of prevention and the damage resulting from the genocide at Srebrenica, financial compensation is not the appropriate form of reparation for the breach of the obligation to prevent genocide'.[36] The Court also declined Bosnia's claim for symbolic compensation, and noted that

> for purposes of reparation, [Serbia's] non-compliance with the provisional measures ordered is an aspect of, or merges with, its breaches of the substantive obligations of prevention and punishment laid upon it by the Convention. The Court does not therefore find it appropriate to give effect to [Bosnia's] request for an order for symbolic compensation in this respect. The Court will however include in the operative clause of the present Judgment, by way of satisfaction, a declaration that [Serbia] has failed to comply with the Court's Orders indicating provisional measures.[37]

The ICJ has also found that injured States who are due reparation should show that restitution is materially impossible or would be disproportionally burdensome. This was the case, for example, in *Jurisdictional Immunities of the State (Germany v. Italy)* in which the Court said

> [i]t has not been alleged or demonstrated that restitution would be materially impossible in this case, or that it would involve a burden

for Italy out of all proportion to the benefit deriving from it. In particular, the fact that some of the violations may have been committed by judicial organs, and some of the legal decisions in question have become final in Italian domestic law, does not lift the obligation incumbent upon Italy to make restitution. On the other hand, the Respondent has the right to choose the means it considers best suited to achieve the required result. Thus, the Respondent is under an obligation to achieve this result by enacting appropriate legislation or by resorting to other methods of its choosing having the same effect.[38]

The ICJ has in fact made three awards of compensation. It first did so in the *Corfu Channel* case.[39] In that case, the UK had claimed compensation for the replacement of a naval vessel, for damage to another vessel as well as for the deaths and injuries of personnel that resulted from the mine explosions. The assessment of the value of these claims put forward by the UK was verified by an expert. As for the replacement of the naval vessel, the Court held that the value was to be the replacement cost of the destroyer at the time of its loss.[40] The UK had claimed GBP700,087 for this head of damage and the Court found this to be justified. As for the damage to the other naval vessel, the expert assessment was marginally less that that initially claimed by the UK, which was GBP93,812. As for the claim in respect of the injured or deceased personnel, the Court granted the UK's claim of GBP50,048, which compensated 'the cost of pensions and other grants made by it to victims or their dependents, and for costs of administration, medical treatment, etc'.[41]

In its deliberations on determining the quantum of compensation in a given case, the Court has introduced a measure of flexibility by referring to equitable considerations as well as what it considers just, fair and reasonable. In the *Diallo* case – the second case in which the ICJ awarded compensation – the Court noted that

> [q]uantification of compensation for non-material injury necessarily rests on equitable considerations . . . which above all involves flexibility and an objective consideration of what is just, fair, and reasonable in all the circumstances of the case, including not only the position of the applicant but the overall context in which the breach occurred.[42]

Many other international courts and tribunals have since referred to the *Chorzów* principle of full reparation. In the Inter-American Court of Human Rights case of *Velasquez Rodriguez*, for example, it was indicated that full reparation meant, 'the restoration of the prior situation, the reparation of the consequences of the violation, and indemnification for patrimonial and non-patrimonial damages, including emotional harm'.[43] The Court also clarified that reparation had to compensate for damage rather than being punitive in nature.[44] The ILC has confirmed this in its Commentary to the Draft Articles on State Responsibility.[45]

The International Tribunal for the Law of the Sea (ITLOS) awarded compensation in its *M/V Saiga (No. 2)* case.[46] In that case, Saint Vincent and the Grenadines had claimed compensation for the wrongful arrest and detention of a vessel and its crew by Guinea. USD2,123,357 with interest was awarded in compensation by ITLOS. The compensation included the costs of repairing damage to the M/V Saiga vessel, the losses that resulted from the inability to charter the vessel and the costs associated with the detention of the vessel, as well as damages caused by the detention of those on board the vessel.[47] However, the compensation that Saint Vincent and the Grenadines had claimed for losing registration revenue as a result of the illegal arrest of the M/V Saiga as well as the cost of the time spent by officials in dealing with the situation were not awarded. As regards the former head of damage, Saint Vincent and the Grenadines had not produced evidence to support their claim. As for the latter head of damage, the tribunal indicated that such activities were within the normal functions of the officials concerned.[48]

The principles developed by courts and tribunals on compensation are largely reflected in the Draft Articles on State Responsibility. Indeed, Article 36 of the Draft Articles on State Responsibility provides that a responsible State must 'compensate for the damage caused thereby, insofar as such damage is not made good by restitution' and that '[t]he compensation shall cover any financially assessable damage including loss of profits insofar as it is established'. The Commentary clarifies that the reference to 'financially assessable damage' excludes 'moral damage' that may be caused to a State, which may include 'the affront or injury caused by a violation of rights not associated with actual damage to property or persons' and which should be remedied by satisfaction.[49] It goes on to highlight that compensation may be for damage sustained by the State, including its property or agents, as well as in lieu of any costs incurred by the State in remedying or mitigating the damage and for damage sustained by nationals of the State, including persons and companies.[50]

Interestingly, Article 27(b) of the Draft Articles on State Responsibility sets out that 'the invocation of a circumstance precluding wrongfulness . . . is without prejudice to . . . the question of compensation for any material loss caused by the act in question'. As such, according to the Draft Articles, even when a circumstance precluding wrongfulness is invoked, compensation may still be due.

Determining the quantum of compensation

Where property rights have been affected by the wrongful action of another State, loss is normally calculated by reference to (1) compensation for capital value, (2) compensation for loss of profits and (3) compensation for incidental expenses.[51] The capital value of property is usually determined on the basis of its 'fair market value'. So, for example, in *American International Group, Inc. v. The Islamic Republic of Iran*, the Iran–US Claims Tribunal noted that 'the valuation should be made on the basis of the fair market value of the shares'.[52] In *Starrett Housing Corporation*, the tribunal conceived fair market value 'as the price that a willing buyer would pay to a willing seller in circumstances in which each had good information, each desired to maximise his financial gain, and neither was under duress or threat'.[53] That said, fair market value may be determined in different ways depending on the asset. This will be easy to determine for assets that are traded regularly on the market but less so for unique goods and services. Businesses can be particularly complex to value, for example. Often tribunals have calculated the value of the business' assets and factored in goodwill and profitability where this was necessary.

Alternatively, capital loss may be determined by net book value. This comprises the difference between the assets and liabilities of a business as is evident from its books. Alternatively again, the discounted cash flow (DCF) method may be used to calculate compensation in some circumstances.[54] It is a method used to estimate the value of an asset in the future based on a projection of how much value it may generate. It has been used to calculate income over a certain period, particularly from wasting assets. Given the inherent speculation involved in income-based methods like DCF, courts and tribunals have preferred to adopt asset-based methods for calculating the value of compensation in commercial contexts.[55]

Lost profits have also been awarded by tribunals in some cases.[56] However, certain tribunals have been cautious in respect of overly speculative claims for loss of profits. In the *Shufeldt* claim, for example, an arbitrator observed that 'the *lucrum cessans* must be the direct fruit of the contract and not too remote or speculative'.[57] Similarly, in *Amco Asia Corporation and Others*, the tribunal allowed non-speculative profits to be recovered.[58] The United Nations Compensation Commission (UNCC) required 'clear and convincing evidence of ongoing and expected profitability' in assessing such claims.[59] Lost profits have not been compensable where the claimant has been unable to establish that they constitute a sufficiently established legally protected interest.[60]

Future profits can be compensated although the threshold is high. Usually the concerned income stream must be developed sufficiently. This may be evidenced by contracts or transactions. The UNCC observed in the context of such claims that

> it is necessary to demonstrate by sufficient documentary and other appropriate evidence a history of successful (i.e. profitable) operation, and a state of affairs which warrants the conclusion that the hypothesis that there would have been future profitable contracts is well founded.[61]

Incidental expenses may also be compensated. These are generally awarded where they have been reasonably incurred in repairing or mitigating damage or loss that results from a wrongful act. The UNCC has awarded compensation for such expenses in respect of evacuation and relief costs, repatriation costs, termination costs, renovation costs and mitigation costs.[62] The Iran–US Claims Tribunal has done so for goods that had to be resold at a loss and for the costs of storage, for example.[63]

Compensation for loss of income has been awarded by a number of international courts and tribunals, including human rights jurisdictions, as well as other compensation mechanisms.[64] While confirming the possibility of compensation for loss of income, the ICJ in the *Diallo* case ultimately rejected Guinea's claim for compensation in lieu of Diallo's loss of earnings while he was detained and following his expulsion based on a lack of evidence and the speculative nature of the amount claimed.[65]

It is widely viewed that compensation under international law cannot be of a punitive or exemplary character.[66] This may prove to be a limitation in the context of environmental damage. Combined with proving a direct causal link, it may prove difficult to assess the amount of tangible damage caused by wrongful behaviour.

Interest is also an important part of ensuring full reparation. The rate of interest and the way in which it is calculated is generally done case-by-case.[67]

Valuing non-pecuniary damage

Various courts and tribunals have assessed non-financial damage as a basis for compensation. For example, in *Lusitania (United States v. Germany)*, a commission adjudged that while certain forms of harm were difficult to quantify, 'the mere fact that they are difficult to measure or estimate by money standards makes them none the less real and affords no reason why the injured person should not be compensated therefor as compensatory damages'.[68] In this case, the umpire referred to 'mental suffering, injury to feelings, humiliation, shame, degradation, loss of social position or injury to his credit or to his reputation'.[69]

Another example is provided by the Inter-American Court of Human Rights in the case of *Gutiérrez-Soler v. Colombia* in which it states that '[n]on pecuniary damage may include distress, suffering, tampering with the victim's core values, and changes of a non-pecuniary nature in the person's everyday life'.[70] In *Diallo*, the ICJ states that 'non-material injury can be established even without specific evidence'[71] and that '[q]uantification of compensation for non-material injury necessarily rests on equitable considerations'. In *Al-Jedda v. United Kingdom*, the European Court of Human Rights was of the view that

> Its guiding principle is equity, which above all involves flexibility and an objective consideration of what is just, fair and reasonable in all the circumstances of the case, including not only the position of the applicant but the overall context in which the breach occurred. Its non-pecuniary awards serve to give recognition to the fact that moral damage occurred as a result of a breach of a fundamental human right and reflect in the broadest of terms the severity of the damage. . . . In the light of all the circumstances of the present case, the Court considers that, to compensate each of the first five applicants for the distress caused by the lack of a fully independent investigation into the deaths of their relatives, it would be just and equitable to award the full amount claimed.[72]

Moreover, the Inter-American Court of Human Rights has also referred to the discretion a court has in assessing damages as well as that a determination be made on the basis of equity.[73] Finally, the jurisprudence of human rights bodies is also replete with examples of valuing non-pecuniary damage such as personal injury. Such bodies usually quantify non-material damage by reference to equitable considerations.[74]

Despite the apparent difficulties of calculating such compensation, courts and tribunals have nevertheless adopted methods to do so. For example, a formula used by Umpire Parker in the previously mentioned *Lusitania* case to appraise the value of compensation for wrongful death has become well known:

> Estimate the amounts (a) which the decedent, had he not been killed, would probably have contributed to the claimant, add thereto (b) the pecuniary value to such claimant of the deceased's personal services in claimant's care, education, or supervision, and also add (c) reasonable compensation for such mental suffering or shock, if any, caused by the violent severing of family ties, as claimant may actually have sustained by reason of such death. The sum of these estimates reduced

to its present cash value, will generally represent the loss sustained by the claimant.[75]

In other cases, compensation for wrongful deprivation of liberty has been calculated by reference to the number of days a victim was detained, and more compensation was awarded where the detained was subjected to confinement or physical or psychological abuse.[76]

Concluding remarks

Article 36 of the Draft Articles confirms that compensation is a secondary means of reparation. Indeed, restitution has 'primacy as a matter of legal principle' but may be substituted by compensation (or another form of reparation) where restitution cannot be ordered for the reasons set out in Article 35 of the Draft Articles. It is generally understood that the responsible State should compensate for any financially assessable losses or damage.[77] Moreover, damages are in general subject to causation, remoteness, evidentiary requirements and principles of accounting, all of which seek to ensure speculative elements are discounted.[78] Similarly, tribunals will seek to avoid double-recovery while nevertheless ensuring full reparation. Furthermore, where the injured party fails to mitigate damages or is liable for contributory fault, this will likely limit the quantum of compensation.[79]

However, as this exploration has revealed, courts and tribunals have been able to value non-financial damages, including for violations of human rights or moral damages. They have also had recourse to considerations of equity in determining the value of non-financial damages as well as, more generally, assessing quantum where it is appropriate that such considerations be applied. We will consider the methods used in determining the quantum of compensation for environmental damages, including in the case law of domestic and international tribunals, later in the next chapters.

Notes

1   *Corfu Channel Case (Assessment of the Amount of Compensation Due from the People's Republic of Albania to the United Kingdom of Great Britain and Northern Ireland)* [1949] ICJ Rep 244; *Case Concerning Ahmadou Sadio Diallo (Republic of Guinea v. Democratic Republic of the Congo)*, Compensation, Judgment [2012] ICJ Rep 324; *Certain Activities Carried Out By Nicaragua in the Border Area (Costa Rica v. Nicaragua) (Compensation)*, ICJ General List No. 150 (2 February 2018).

2   This is also known as the *Chorzów* formula: *Factory at Chorzów*, Jurisdiction [1927] PCIJ Series A, No. 9, 21 and *Factory at Chorzów*, Merits [1928] PCIJ Series A, No. 9, 47.

3 Draft Articles on the Responsibility of States for Internationally Wrongful Acts II(2) YBILC (2001), 91.
4 Ibid., 91–2.
5 Ibid., 92.
6 *Corfu Channel Case*, op cit.
7 Ibid.
8 *United States Diplomatic and Consular Staff in Tehran* [1980] ICJ Rep 3.
9 Draft Articles on the Responsibility of States for Internationally Wrongful Acts, Commentaries, op cit, 93.
10 See, for example, *D. Earnshaw and Others (Great Britain) v. United States (Zafiro case)* VI [1925] Reports of International Arbitral Awards 160, 164–5.
11 Francisco de Vitoria, 'Second Relectio: On the Indians [1538–1539]' in J. Brown Scott (ed.), *The Spanish Origins of International Law: Francisco de Vitoria and His Law of Nations* (Clarendon Press, 1934), Appendix B.
12 Hugo Grotius, *De Jure Belli Ac Pacis* [1625], *Liber secundus, caput* XVII (Nijhoff, 1948), 79–82.
13 Samuel Pufendorf, *Elementorum Jurisprudentiae Universalis–Libri Duo* 1672 (University of Lausanne, 2010).
14 Ibid.
15 See Christian Wolff, *Principes du droit de la nature et des gens* 1758 (Presses Universitaires de Caen, 2011), Book IX, 293–4 and 296; Christian Wolff, *Jus Gentium Methodo Scientica Pertractatum* 1764 (Clarendon Press, 1934), 162.
16 See *Diallo*, op cit, Seperate Opinion: Judge Cançado Trindade, para 25.
17 *Chorzów Factory*, Merits, op cit.
18 Ibid., para 125.
19 Ibid., para 142.
20 *Norwegian Shipowner's Claims (Norway v. US)* VI [1922] Reports of International Arbitral Awards 309.
21 *Rainbow Warrior Case (New Zealand v. France)* 74 [1990] Reports of International Arbitral Awards 215, 251.
22 *Case Concerning the Gabčikovo-Nagymaros Project (Hungary/Slovakia)* [1997] ICJ Rep 7.
23 Ibid.
24 Ibid.
25 See, for example, *Diallo*, op cit, para 14; *Costa Rica v. Nicaragua (Compensation)*, op cit, para 72.
26 Juan José Quintana, *Litigation at the International Court of Justice: Practice and Procedure* (Brill, 2015), 1176.
27 *Fisheries Jurisdiction (Germany v. Iceland)* [1974] ICJ Rep 175, para 76.
28 *Military and Paramilitary Activities in and against Nicaragua (Nicaragua v. US)*, Merits [1986] ICJ Rep 14.
29 *United States Diplomatic and Consular Staff in Tehran*, op cit, para 95.
30 *Armed Activities on the Territory of the Congo (Democratic Republic of the Congo v. Uganda)*, Judgment [2005] ICJ Rep 168.
31 *Certain Activities Carried Out By Nicaragua in the Border Area (Costa Rica v. Nicaragua) and Construction of a Road in Costa Rica along the San Juan River (Nicaragua v. Costa Rica)*, Judgment [2015] ICJ Rep 665.
32 *Legal Consequences of the Construction of a Wall in the Occupied Palestinian Territory*, Advisory Opinion [2004] ICJ Rep 136.
33 Ibid., para 153.

34 Draft Articles on the Responsibility of States for Internationally Wrongful Acts, Commentaries, op cit, 99.
35 *Application of the Convention on the Prevention and Punishment of the Crime of Genocide (Bosnia & Herzegovina v. Serbia & Montenegro)*, Judgment [2007] ICJ Rep 43, para 479.
36 Ibid., para 462.
37 Ibid., para 469.
38 *Jurisdictional Immunities of the State (Germany v. Italy)* [2012] ICJ Rep 99, para 137.
39 *Corfu Channel Case*, op cit.
40 Ibid.
41 Ibid., 249.
42 *Diallo*, op cit, para 24.
43 *Velásquez Rodríguez Case* 4 [1988] Inter-Am.Ct.H.R. Ser. C.
44 Ibid., 225.
45 Draft Articles on the Responsibility of States for Internationally Wrongful Acts, Commentaries, op cit, 99.
46 *M/V Saiga (No. 2) Case (Saint Vincent and the Grenadines v. Guinea)*, Judgment [1999] ITLOS Rep 10.
47 Ibid.
48 Ibid., para 177.
49 Draft Articles on the Responsibility of States for Internationally Wrongful Acts, Commentaries, op cit, 99.
50 Ibid.
51 Ibid., 102.
52 *American International Group, Inc. v. The Islamic Republic of Iran* 4 [1983] Iran-U.S.C.T.R. 96, 106.
53 *Starrett Housing Corporation v. The Islamic Republic of Iran* 16 [1987] Iran-U.S.C.T.R. 112, 201.
54 See *Amoco International Finance Corporation; Starrett Housing Corporation; Phillips Petroleum Company Iran; and Ebrahimi (Shahin Shaine) v. Islamic Republic of Iran* 30 [1994] Iran-U.S.C.T.R. 170.
55 Draft Articles on the Responsibility of States for Internationally Wrongful Acts, Commentaries, op cit, 104.
56 See, for example, *Sapphire International Petroleums Ltd. v. National Iranian Oil Company* 35 [1963] ILR 136, 187 and 189; *Amco Asia Corporation and Others v. The Republic of Indonesia*, First Arbitration [1984]; Annulment [1986]; Resubmitted case [1990], 1 ICSID Reports (Cambridge, Grotius, 1993), 377; and *AGIP SpA v. the Government of the People's Republic of the Congo* [1979] 1 ICSID Reports (Cambridge, Grotius, 1993), 306.
57 *Shufeldt Claim (Guatemala, USA)* II [1930] Reports of International Arbitral Awards 1079, 1099.
58 *Amco Asia Corporation and Others*, ICSID/ARB./81/1, 612.
59 UNCC, *Report and Recommendations Made By the Panel of Commissioners Concerning the First Instalment of 'E3' Claims* (17 December 1998) (S/AC.26/1998/13), para 147.
60 See, for example, *The Oscar Chinn Case (Britain v. Belgium)* [1934] PCIJ Series A/B, No. 63; *Asian Agricultural Products, Final Award* (27 June 1990), ICSID Case No. ARB/87/3.

61 UNCC, *Report and Recommendations Made By the Panel of Commissioners Concerning the Fourth Instalment of 'E3' Claims* (30 September 1999), UN Doc. S/AC.26/1999/14, para 140.

62 See UNCC, *Report and Recommendations Made By the Panel of Commissioners Concerning the First Instalment of 'E2' Claims* (3 July 1998), UN Doc. S/AC.26/1998/7.

63 *General Electric Company v. The Government of the Islamic Republic of Iran*, 26 [1991] Iran-U.S.C.T.R. 148, paras 56–60 and 67–9.

64 See, for example, *Teixeira de Castro v. Portugal*, Application No. 44/1997/828/1034, Judgment [1998] ECHR Rep IV, paras 46–9; *Suárez-Rosero v. Ecuador*, Judgment on reparations and costs [1999] IACHR, Series C, No. 44, para 60; UNCC, *Report and Recommendations Made By the Panel of Commissioners Concerning the Fourteenth Instalment of 'E3' Claims* (29 September 2000), UN Doc. S/AC.26/2000/19, para 126.

65 *Diallo*, op cit, para 49.

66 *Costa Rica v. Nicaragua (Compensation)*, op cit, para 31.

67 *The 'Wimbledon' (Government of His Britannic Majesty et al v. German Empire)* [1923] PCIJ Series A, No. 1, 32; *M/V Saiga*, op cit, para 173; *Case A19 (Iran v United States)*, Decision 16 [1986] Iran-U.S.C.T.R 285, 289–90.

68 United States-Germany Mixed Claims Commission, *Opinion in the Lusitania Cases*, VII [1923] Reports of International Arbitral Awards, 32, 40.

69 Ibid.

70 *Gutiérrez-Soler v. Colombia*, Merits, Reparations and Costs [2005] IACtHR Series C, No. 132, para 82.

71 *Diallo*, op cit, para 21.

72 *Al-Jedda v. United Kingdom*, Application No. 27021/08, Judgment [2011] ECHR, para 114.

73 *Cantoral Benavides v. Peru*, Judgment, Reparations and Costs [2001] IACtHR Series C, No. 88, para 53.

74 Draft Articles on the Responsibility of States for Internationally Wrongful Acts, Commentaries, 102. See also, Dinah Shelton, *Remedies in International Human Rights Law* (Oxford University Press, 1999).

75 *Lusitania*, op cit, 35.

76 See, for example, *The 'Topaze' Case*, IX [1903] Reports of International Arbitral Awards 387, 389; *The Faulkner Case*, IV [1926] Reports of International Arbitral Awards 67, 71; *The William McNeil Case*, V [1931] Reports of International Arbitral Awards 164, 168.

77 *Lusitania*, op cit.

78 Draft Articles on the Responsibility of States for Internationally Wrongful Acts, Commentaries, 105.

79 *Case Concerning the Gabčikovo-Nagymaros Project*, op cit, 80.

2 Environmental compensation in the practice of international courts and tribunals

Introduction

In this chapter, we will home in on approaches to awarding compensation for environmental damage at the international level. The complexity of the environment means that the traditional principles of compensation in international law are challenged. For example, can compensation be full or fair and adequate if it only reimburses material losses or costs incurred? Furthermore, questions around causation, contribution, significance and valuation tend to be more difficult to address in this context.

The commentary to Article 36 of the Draft Articles on State Responsibility provides an overview of the parameters of compensation for environmental damage in practice, including that payments have been made to injured States as a means of reimbursing expenses reasonably incurred in preventing or remedying pollution or to compensate a reduction in the value of property.[1] However, the Commentary also appears to recognise that compensation for environmental damage may extend beyond such parameters and include aspects like biodiversity, amenity or other 'non-use' values. How this squares with conventional and case law on the matter will be examined.

Recent years have seen a marked trend in the award of monetary compensation for environmental damage.[2] However, in many cases, international courts and tribunals have made questionable methodological choices. Moreover, they have mostly rejected the methods proposed by State parties in the litigation and, on occasion, appointed their own experts to appraise environmental damage. Further still, given the opacity in some of the reasoning of international courts and tribunals in this context, it is far from clear how an international tribunal might calculate compensation for environmental damage in future cases. This chapter will engage with the judgments and awards of different international courts and tribunals, critically appraising the methodologies adopted and approaches taken.

The International Court of Justice and environmental compensation

The decision of the ICJ in its *Question of Compensation (Costa Rica v. Nicaragua)* case of 2 February 2018 provides a pioneering example of damage to the environment being litigated before an international tribunal. The judgment is the first time that the ICJ has adjudicated compensation for environmental damage, and it is only the third time the ICJ has awarded compensation at all.[3] Nevertheless, the ICJ boldly asserted in this case that 'damage to the environment, and the consequent impairment or loss of the ability of the environment to provide goods and services, is compensable under international law'.[4] That said, the reasoning employed by the Court leaves much to be desired. Given the increasing number of cases involving the environment, it is unfortunate that international courts and tribunals will garner only limited guidance from the methodology adopted by the ICJ in valuing environmental damage.

As for the background to this judgment, Costa Rica instituted proceedings against Nicaragua in 2010, alleging incursion, occupation and use of its territory by Nicaragua, as well as breaches by Nicaragua of treaty obligations owed to Costa Rica. After joining these proceedings with those in the *Construction of a Road in Costa Rica along the San Juan River (Nicaragua v. Costa Rica)*, concerning transboundary harm caused by Costa Rica, the Court handed down its judgment on the merits on 16 December 2015.[5]

In the joined cases, the Court found that Costa Rica had sovereignty over the disputed territory and that Nicaragua must compensate Costa Rica for material damage to the environment resulting from its unlawful activities on the territory. If the parties could not agree on the amount of compensation within 12 months of the judgment, compensation would be settled by the Court.[6] The parties could not reach an agreement and Costa Rica asked the ICJ to resolve the issue of compensation.

In their respective pleadings on the compensation owed, each of the parties put forward different methodologies for calculating the environmental damage in monetary terms. Costa Rica suggested an 'ecosystem services approach', while Nicaragua suggested a 'replacement costs approach'. As a result of these differing methodologies, the parties came to significantly different conclusions as to the amount of compensation owed. Costa Rica estimated that environmental damages amounted to approximately USD6.711 million while Nicaragua arrived at an amount of USD188,504.[7]

An ecosystem services approach to valuing environmental damage

According to Costa Rica's 'ecosystem services approach' the environment is valued by reference to the goods and services that make it up. Some goods and services may be traded on the market and have a 'direct use value' (e.g., timber) while other goods and services cannot be traded on the market and have an 'indirect use value' (e.g., flood prevention). Ecosystem or environmental services are various services that may be lost as a result of damage to the environment. This may comprise provisioning services (e.g., food, fibre, wood, fuel or medicines), regulating services (e.g., biological retention, freshwater storage and retention, water regulation, climate, atmosphere and gas regulation, human disease control, flood and storm protection, erosion control and waste treatment), cultural services or supporting services (which support other ecosystem services).

Costa Rica then used a value transfer approach to give the damaged environmental goods and services a monetary value. This involved assessing the value of ecosystems having similar conditions – that is tropical coastal wetland – or using a direct valuation of the concerned ecosystem where such data was available. Once the value of the loss in the first year the damage was caused had been calculated, a net present value calculation for the following 50 years with a discount rate of 4% was adopted.

This approach, Costa Rica claimed, reflected the full extent of environmental damage and found support in international and domestic practice. It also argued that it was the most appropriate methodology for a protected wetland and consistent with its commitments under the Ramsar Convention. As for the calculation, a 'total value equation' was used to calculate direct use values (e.g., commercial or consumptive values) and indirect values (e.g., natural or cultural capital services). This equation has been used by the United Nations Environment Programme as well as the Ramsar Secretariat.[8]

A replacement costs approach to valuing environmental damage

Under Nicaragua's 'replacement costs approach', the cost of preserving an equivalent area while the affected area recovers is the value to be used to calculate the compensation owed. Additional ecological services replace those that have been damaged. Nicaragua argued that its approach tracked the method used most frequently by the United Nations Compensation Commission (UNCC) for valuing environmental damage in the first Gulf War. Nicaragua also accepted that Costa Rica may be entitled to restoration costs, which are the expenses incurred as a result of remediation works. For Nicaragua, Costa Rica should only be compensated for the purchase of an area equivalent to that damaged, as well as the costs of certain remediation work.

An overall valuation approach to valuing environmental damage

After having considered the suggested approaches of the parties, the Court made a general point of principle: it is consistent with international law, especially in light of the need to ensure full reparation, to order compensation for damage to the environment. For the Court, international law permits compensation for both environmental damage and for the costs and expenses incurred by Costa Rica arising from Nicaragua's unlawful activities (e.g., monitoring and restoration of the damaged environment). While the approaches put forward by both parties had precedents, the Court noted that there was also precedent for other methods of calculating compensation. As a result, the Court reasoned that it would not choose between the two methodologies set out by the parties, but rather '[w]herever certain elements of either method offer a reasonable basis for valuation, the Court [would] nonetheless take them into account'.[9]

Ultimately, the Court decided to value environmental damage based on what it called an 'overall valuation approach'. Using this approach, compensation for environmental damage is calculated based on an overall evaluation of the impairment or loss of environmental goods and services, rather than by calculating the value of specific categories of environmental goods and services as well as the time it may take each to recover. The Court applied this methodology to the claim for damage to the environment. It would apply a different methodology later in its judgment to calculate compensation for the costs incurred by Costa Rica resulting from Nicaragua's unlawful activities, which included the cost of monitoring and repairing the environmental damage.

The Court's stated reasons for choosing the 'overall valuation' methodology are worth noting. First, it was keen to adopt an approach that accounted for the correlation between the activities of Nicaragua and the harm caused to certain environmental goods and services. Second, it considered its approach more appropriate than others in light of the specific characteristics of the area affected, namely a protected wetland under the Ramsar Convention with closely interlinked environmental goods and services. Third, an overall valuation allowed the Court to take into account the capacity of the damaged area for natural regeneration. The Court also referred to the *Chorzów* formula that 'the breach of an engagement involves an obligation to make reparation in an adequate form' and, accordingly, an injured party should be repaired in such a way that they are put back in the same position as if the illegal act had not occurred.[10] However, the Court is not clear on why the overall valuation approach serves these aims better than the other methodologies considered. We can only assume the Court deemed those other methodologies to be either over- or under-inclusive.

A close reading of the judgment suggests that the Court's overall valuation approach was influenced by an alternative valuation offered by Nicaragua in its pleadings, the so-called 'corrected analysis'. The 'corrected analysis' applies Costa Rica's ecosystem services approach but with significant adjustments to the categories of environmental goods and services included and the values used. Despite critiquing this 'corrected analysis' in paragraph 85 of its judgment, the Court seemingly goes on to apply a variation of the 'corrected analysis' for the purpose of arriving at its overall valuation in paragraph 86. While noting that the absence of certainty should not preclude it from awarding an amount approximately reflecting the environmental damage caused, the Court considered that, 'for the purposes of its overall valuation, an adjustment be made to the total amount in the "corrected analysis" to account for the shortcomings'.[11]

As a way of justifying the potential uncertainties in the valuation of environmental damage, the Court referred to *Diallo*, a case in which 'equitable considerations' were drawn upon to determine the amount of compensation.[12] This also allowed the Court room to take into account the particular contexts in which the parties found themselves. Moreover, it cited the *Trail Smelter* case,[13] which in turn refers to a US Supreme Court decision[14] stating that, 'where the tort itself is of such a nature as to preclude the ascertainment of the amount of damages with certainty, it would be a perversion of fundamental principles of justice to deny all relief to the injured person' and that, as such 'it will be enough if the evidence show the extent of damages as a matter of just and reasonable interference, although the result be only approximate'.[15]

Before actually calculating the compensation owed, the Court sought to appraise the existence and extent of the damage as well as establish whether there existed a direct and certain causal link between the environmental harm and Nicaragua's wrongful acts. Similarly, in the latter part of the judgment assessing the costs and expenses that Costa Rica claimed it incurred from its restoration and monitoring activities, the Court placed an emphasis on the existence of a direct connection with the wrongful actions of Nicaragua. Where a link between the incurred cost and the wrongful act was lacking, the Court rejected compensation for the cost (e.g., aircraft insurance or the regular wages of government employees).

Lastly, the Court considered whether pre- and post-judgment interest could be applied to the principal amount of compensation, as argued by Costa Rica. The Court concluded that interest was payable at a rate of 4% per annum in the pre-judgment period and at a rate of 6% per annum in the post-judgment period should Nicaragua fail to pay the compensation due by April 2018.

The Court finally awarded total compensation in the amount of USD378,890.59, including pre-judgment interest, and Nicaragua has since paid this compensation.[16]

An analysis of the ICJ's first decision on environmental compensation

The Court's judgment is both significant and innovative for awarding compensation for environmental damage. The decision is also notable for its bold statements of principle, opaque methodological choices, some internal contradiction and for awarding much lower valuations for environmental damage than the claimant had argued. Indeed, the amount awarded represented around 5% of the claim made by Costa Rica. Without a more detailed account of its environmental damage valuation methodology as well as the application of its nexus test to incurred costs and expenses, it is difficult to appraise whether the Court was justified in awarding this lower amount. Several aspects of the judgment can, however, be analysed more deeply.

First, the Court confirms that damage to the environment *itself* is compensable under international law. For the Court, environmental damage includes the inability of the environment to provide goods and services. This is distinct from the expenses incurred by a State as a result of such damage, which can also be compensable and include remediation and monitoring costs. In addition to its bold affirmation, the ICJ's judgment clarifies several concrete matters related to the calculation of compensation. For example, the ICJ is open to compensating the wages of officials dealing with the consequences of the wrongful acts of another State where these wages are beyond those budgeted in the ordinary course of events. The ICJ stated that this was 'in line with international practice' and cited a UNCC report.[17] In this way, it would appear that the Court made a distinction between variable and fixed costs in certain aspects of its valuation methodology.

Second, the opinion involves some opaque methodology. On the issue of interest, the Court stated that 'pre-judgment interest may be awarded if full reparation for injury caused by an internationally wrongful act so requires'.[18] That said, the Court tempered this statement by observing that 'interest is not an autonomous form of reparation, nor is it a necessary part of compensation in every case'.[19] The Court then made a curious distinction in awarding pre-judgment interest on the compensation for Costa Rica's restoration and monitoring costs but not on the compensation for environmental damage. On this issue, the Court noted it had 'taken full account of the impairment or loss of environmental goods and services in the period prior to recovery' and, as such, did not need to apply pre-judgment interest to the compensation for environmental damage.[20] However, the Court said post-judgment interest would apply on both environmental damage and costs and expenses incurred by Costa Rica if Nicaragua did not pay the compensation ordered within the time limit it stipulated. To support this conclusion, the Court simply referred to the *Diallo* case, in which it reasoned that 'the award of post-judgment interest is consistent with the practice of other international courts and tribunals'.[21] The ICJ saw no reason to deviate from this approach in the present case.[22] The method by which the Court arrived at its interest calculations is, however, as opaque as its method for calculating the principal sum of compensation owed.

Indeed, it is far from clear how an international tribunal might calculate environmental damage in future cases based on this decision by the ICJ. While it seems appropriate to adopt a flexible approach to the calculation of compensation, leaving room to tailor a methodology to the circumstances of a given case, the Court unfortunately does not adequately explain the particulars of the methodology it used. This opacity makes it very difficult to critically assess the application of the methodology adopted by the Court, and it provides no authoritative touchstone for other international courts or tribunals dealing with similar issues.

Despite the lack of clarity, a number of critical observations can nevertheless be made about the methodology. For example, the Court does not explore any baseline environmental assessment prior to Nicaragua causing the damage. This omission comes into particularly sharp focus when one recalls the emphasis the ICJ placed on applying the *Chorzów* formula,[23] which aims to put the injured party back in the position it was before the wrongful act took place. The Court also does not give a recovery period estimate or explicitly factor in the cost of mitigation or remediation measures during that recovery period. The categories of environmental goods and services are each very different from one another and should have prompted different methodologies for calculating damage to them. Here, the Court could have referred to other national and international cases that distinguish between different categories of environmental damage, such as clean-up operations performed by public employees, the use of public buildings for the conduct of clean-up operations, restoration activities and the environmental damage caused.[24]

Third, there is some level of contradiction in the Court's judgment. Initially, it gives the impression it wants to apply a methodically clinical valuation approach. For instance, the ICJ emphasised the establishment of a direct and clear nexus between Nicaragua's activities and the environmental damage. Moreover, the judgment suggests that, as a first step, the Court is at pains to assess the existence and extent of the damage prior to calculating the monetary value of that damage. Further still, the Court initially develops an itemised list of what it deems reasonably appropriate to claim for compensation and critiques certain aspects of the detailed methodologies set out by the parties. All of this implied that the Court would ultimately provide a detailed explanation of its favoured valuation methodology. Instead, however, the Court simply embraces a less than clinical 'overall valuation' approach. In doing so, it neither refers to previous practice nor elaborates upon the details of the approach, except to say that it 'can account for the correlation between the removal of the trees and the harm caused to other environmental goods and services',[25] that it 'is dictated by the specific characteristics of the area affected by the activities of Nicaragua'[26] and that it 'take[s] into account the capacity of the damaged area for natural regeneration'.[27] Exactly how and why the overall valuation approach achieves these ends remain a mystery.

Fourth, the ICJ failed to learn from previous litigation on environmental matters. For example, why did the Court not consult experts when assessing the environmental damage? It has this option open to it under Article 50 of the Statute of the ICJ. In fact, in a judgment handed down on the same day as the present case, *Maritime Delimitation in the Caribbean Sea and the Pacific Ocean (Costa Rica v. Nicaragua)*, the Court had appointed its own experts in this way.[28] The resort to experts in scientific matters has also been encouraged by the ICJ in the past, particularly in the *Pulp Mills* case.[29] Moreover, in their Dissenting Opinion in that case, Judges Simma and Al-Khasawneh stressed the importance of referring to experts in cases involving complex scientific matters.[30] Following *Pulp Mills*, scientific experts were resorted to in the *Whaling in the Antarctic* case,[31] as well as in the *Construction of a Road in Costa Rica along the San Juan River* case[32] and in the *Maritime Delimitation in the Caribbean Sea and the Pacific Ocean* case.[33] Further still, although this case is only the third in which the ICJ has awarded inter-State compensation, in both of the prior decisions it appointed its own experts to assess the compensation amount.[34]

To take another example, investor–State dispute settlement tribunals have had recourse to experts in the face of complex counterclaims for environmental damage. In a 2015 International Centre for the Settlement of Investment Disputes (ICSID) case that will be more fully considered later, *Perenco v. Ecuador*,[35] the respondent argued that the claimant had caused environmental damage in the amount of USD3 billion. Recognizing the difficulty in appraising the value of such damage and criticizing the testimony of the parties' experts, the tribunal in that case appointed its own independent environmental expert to assist with the task.[36]

In a further example that will also be considered more fully later, *Burlington Resources Inc. v. Ecuador*, another ICSID tribunal ordered the payment of compensation for environmental damage caused.[37] The Tribunal assessed the harm caused and reparation cost at each of the 40 sites in the oil field exploited by the claimant and even made site visits.

Fifth, whether the conduct of the parties in a given case should be accounted for in assessments of compensation is another important aspect to clarify. While many agree that it is not possible to award punitive damages under international law, others suggest that it is possible to factor in elements such as gravely wrongful conduct, the degree of fault, intention, bad faith or negligence in a calculation of compensation. Similarly, certain courts and tribunals have confirmed that punitive compensation is not permitted under international law,[38] while other international tribunals have nevertheless awarded relief that takes into account the egregious behaviour of a party.[39] Moreover, the ILC and the *Institut de droit international* have both indicated that the behaviour of the parties is relevant to the evaluation of compensation, as are considerations of equity.[40] Dissenting ICJ judges in the *Question of Compensation* case suggested the gravity of Nicaragua's wrongful behaviour should have been taken into account in the assessment of damages.[41]

In the final analysis, this case is part of an emerging trend towards the environment becoming a more regular feature of international adjudication.[42] Despite the flaws in the judgment of the ICJ in the *Question of Compensation* case, it is significant that the Court – the principal judicial organ of the United Nations – found environmental damage itself to be compensable, at least in the form of goods and services provided by the environment. We now turn to consider other recent cases in which environmental compensation has been awarded.

Environmental compensation in investor–State dispute settlement awards

The emerging practice of awarding environmental compensation is also evident in several investor–State disputes. In *Burlington Resources v. Ecuador*, for example, an ICSID tribunal ordered the payment of USD41 million in compensation for environmental damage caused by the Claimant.[43] It did so on the basis of Ecuadorian national law, but the methodology adopted by the tribunal is worthy of consideration.

Burlington Resources is a US company investing in several oil production facilities in Ecuador together with its consortium partner Perenco Ecuador Ltd (Perenco). Burlington was assigned production-sharing contracts (PSCs) in 2001. The PSCs put the entire cost and operational risk on Burlington and Perenco. In return, they were to receive a share in the oil produced. The PSCs defined the tax regime applicable to Burlington. Ecuador subsequently adopted laws that raised taxes on oil companies for an 'unforeseen' rise of oil prices in excess of the price level at the time of conclusion of the PSCs. Burlington initially paid the additional tax but later stopped paying it. After Burlington threatened to stop the production, Ecuador took possession of the oil production facilities in 2009. Ecuador ultimately annulled the PSCs with Burlington by ministerial decree.

Burlington made a Request for ICSID Arbitration and argued that four measures taken by Ecuador – the laws, the seizure of shares, the physical takeover of the production facilities and the termination of the PSCs – constituted expropriation. According to Ecuador, its measures were not expropriatory mainly because Burlington had no right to revenues stemming from oil prices in excess of the price assumption made by the parties. In addition, Ecuador filed counterclaims for violations of Ecuadorian environmental laws and breaches of contractual obligations by Burlington. Counterclaims are increasingly used a means for challenging an investor's implementation of their obligations in investor–State dispute settlement.

In its decision on liability, by analysing each measure individually, the tribunal found that the tax law was not expropriatory as such because it did not substantially deprive Burlington of the investment as a whole. The seizure of certain fractions of the investment was also not tantamount to expropriation mainly because the investment remained profitable. However, the tribunal found that Ecuador expropriated Burlington's investment when it took possession of the production facilities.

During the case, the tribunal made site visits to assess '(i) soil contamination, including issues of topography and groundwater and (ii) land use, including the Sumaco Biosphere Reserve'.[44] At each of the sites, the parties' counsel were permitted to make oral presentations as well as to answer any questions that the tribunal had.

Subsequently, the tribunal issued a decision on the counterclaims made by Ecuador, ordering Burlington to pay Ecuador for breaches of Ecuadorian environmental law and contractual obligations. According to Ecuadorian law, Burlington was strictly liable for environmental damage. In its quantification of compensation, the tribunal applied a strict liability remediation costs approach under Ecuadorian domestic law. The tribunal also assessed the notion of environmental harm. Burlington argued that 'environmental harm is defined by reference to "permissible limits" set out in applicable regulations' while Ecuador referred to '"background values" that reflect environmental conditions as they were prior to any human interference'. The tribunal was of the view that

> [p]roper environmental stewardship has assumed great importance in today's world [and] that if a legal relationship between an investor and the State permits the filing of a claim by the State for environmental damage caused by the investor's activities and such a claim is substantiated, the State is entitled to full reparation.[45]

In a separate but factually connected case, *Perenco v. Ecuador*,[46] Ecuador argued through a counterclaim that the claimant had caused environmental damage in the amount of USD3 billion by polluting parts of the Amazon rainforest from the same oil production facilities we have just considered in the *Burlington* case. Recognizing the difficulty in appraising the value of such damage and criticizing the testimony of the parties' experts, the *Perenco* tribunal appointed its own independent environmental expert to assist with the task.[47] Having reviewed all of the evidence put forward by the parties and the tribunal-appointed expert, the tribunal was of the view that Perenco would likely be liable for causing environmental damage. As such, in an Interim Decision, the tribunal declined to decide the specific aspects of the counterclaim but suggested it would do so in the final decision, and it is likely that the tribunal's expert will value the damage.[48]

Interestingly, the *Perenco* and *Burlington* tribunals diverged on their interpretation of whether Ecuadorian law provided for a fault-based or strict-liability regime for environmental harm. The *Burlington* tribunal said

> it has difficulty following the *Perenco* tribunal's view that decisions of the Ecuadorian courts have merely 'strengthened the presumptions in favour of a finding of liability in the case of damage caused through hazardous activities' [and] finds indeed that these courts have established a strict liability regime for hazardous activities, in particular oilfield operations.[49]

In *David Aven et al v. Costa Rica*, another investor–State dispute settlement tribunal found that the Claimants had breached environmental laws in Costa Rica and that Costa Rica had justifiably interfered with a tourism project investment on the grounds of environmental protection.[50] David Aven et al. made their claim under the Dominican Republic-Central America Free Trade Agreement (DR-CAFTA). They argued that they had received the required permits and approvals, including those related to the environmental viability of the project. However, following subsequent inspection of the site, Claimants argued that administrative and judicial actions were taken to shut down the project to avoid environmental harm to wetlands and forests. According to Claimants, this destroyed the investment and breached the DR-CAFTA's provisions on fair and equitable treatment, non-discrimination and expropriation.

Costa Rica responded that environmental protection was a policy that could be legitimately pursued under the DR-CAFTA, that environmental protection could be prioritised above the rights of investors and that it acted in accordance with domestic environmental law in order to protect its environment and ecosystems. Costa Rica went on to submit a counterclaim against the Claimants for a violation of the provisions on environmental protection under the DR-CAFTA. Indeed, it requested the tribunal to order that Claimants pay damages to Costa Rica for the purpose of restoring the situation that existed prior to Claimants' wrongful impact on the concerned wetland.[51]

The tribunal was of the view that Costa Rica did not act in an arbitrary way and had not violated the DR-CAFTA. The Claimants had damaged the environment and Costa Rica had acted to protect the wetland at risk. It had done so in accordance with municipal and international law. Moreover, it found that counterclaims for environmental damage could be established under the DR-CAFTA. However, the tribunal ultimately rejected Costa Rica's counterclaim for procedural reasons. In particular, Costa Rica had not properly presented its claim for environmental damage and only attempted to rectify the lack of detail in its submissions after the deadline set by the tribunal. The tribunal commented that:

> Costa Rica only made a general reference to environmental damages in the Las Olas Project site attributed to the Claimants' activity. There is no precise statement of the facts supporting the claims but rather a reference to expert reports attached to those pleadings. There is no specification of the relief sought but in very general terms and the quantification is much approximated, based only in the personal experience of an expert rather than any accurate method of valuation.[52]

Notwithstanding, the tribunal noted that 'environmental law is integrated in many ways to international law, including DR-CAFTA'[53] and that while it was for States to implement appropriate environmental law, foreign investors were also subject to particular obligations in relation to the environment as set out under the treaty at hand and international law. Moreover, Section A of Article 10 of the DR-CAFTA provides that investors are under an obligation to comply with measures taken at the national level for environmental protection, and the tribunal observed that there are no 'substantive reasons to exempt [a] foreign investor of the scope of claims for breaching obligations under Article 10 Section A DR-CAFTA, particularly in the field of environmental law'.[54]

Counterclaims therefore appear to be a promising avenue for States to pursue compensation for environmental damage caused by foreign investors. Despite their recent appearance in a number of cases, however, there remain a number of uncertainties that persist around the practice of counterclaims. Whether these need to be explicitly provided for in a treaty and the extent to which the counterclaim should be connected to the principal claim are matters that need to be clarified. Some tribunals have taken the approach that parties should have consented to the exercise of counterclaims, evidence for which may be found in the treaty's arbitration clause.[55] Other approaches look towards the arbitral rules for a possibility to introduce counterclaims.[56] This is the reason that their explicit provision in international investment instruments, as has been the case with the COMESA Investment Agreement, the SADC Model BIT and the Draft Pan-African Investment Code, for example, helps to bring clarity for States and investors alike.

In a similar way, treaties having environmental obligations for investors is a promising way to allow investment tribunals to consider such matters. Other options may be through domestic law or contractual obligations that become internationalised via an international investment agreement's legality requirements or applicable law clause and the Vienna Convention on the Law of Treaties' systemic integration provision.[57]

Broadening notions of environmental harm

Several recent cases in international courts and tribunals, particularly human rights courts, suggest that understandings of environmental harm are broadening. In particular, the connection between environmental degradation and the deprivation of human rights has been underlined. In a significant advisory opinion, the Inter-American Court of Human Rights in its *The Environment and Human Rights* case[58] confirmed the link between the realisation of human rights and the existence of a healthy environment. The Court found that States should take measures to ensure significant environmental harm is not caused to individuals within or beyond their territory.[59] In establishing a justiciable right to a healthy environment under the American Convention on Human Rights, this Opinion may well open the door for individual litigants to bring a case where this right has been interfered with, even extraterritorially. This is especially relevant in the context of growing climate litigation at the domestic and regional levels, as will be explored further in Chapter 4.

In the case, Colombia had asked the Court to opine on three main questions. The first question was whether the term 'jurisdiction' under Article 1(1) of the American Convention on Human Rights would permit an individual living in one State to bring a claim for violations of human rights resulting from environmental harm caused by another State. As for the second question, assuming a positive response to that first question, it asked whether serious transboundary environmental damage caused by a State could constitute a breach of the rights to life and personal integrity under the Convention. The third question was whether respect for the Convention requires State parties to abide by international environmental law. The Court mostly answered these questions affirmatively. What is more, several States in the region, including Guatemala, Honduras and Bolivia, submitted observations to the Court that advocated for affirmative answers to those questions.[60]

Suggesting extra-territorial reach, the Court asserted that the jurisdiction of a State can extend beyond its territory where activities conducted within its territory have cross-border effects.[61] Moreover, the Court noted that States have a duty to ensure the rights of persons outside their territory are not impaired.[62] It thus offers an expanded notion of jurisdiction.[63] In this respect, a stronger argument can now be made that greenhouse gases emitted by a State could lead to the attribution of responsibility for damage caused to people in other States. It has been said that this case contributes to the evolving case law on 'cross border human rights claims arising from transboundary environmental impacts',[64] and it will be interesting to see if this innovative interpretation of jurisdiction, a common limitation in the applicability of human rights treaties, may be followed in other contexts.

Another case of the Inter-American Court of Human Rights, *Kaliña and Lokono Peoples v. Suriname*, concerned environmental damage caused to the land of an indigenous community.[65] Of interest in this case was that the Court ordered, amongst other reparation, compensation for damage caused to 'the environment and the lands of the Kaliña and Lokono peoples owing to the bauxite mining operations in the Wane Kreek Nature Reserve'.[66] It thus offers an example of a human rights court awarding compensation for environmental damage.

Similarly, the European Court of Human Rights in *López Ostra v. Spain* held that, where a State fails to control industrial pollution, this can amount to a violation of Article 8 of the European Convention on Human Rights where there is sufficiently grave interference with an individual's home and private life.[67] In that case, the Court considered that it had to balance the economic interest of the community concerned in industrial activities with the interests of an individual.

The applicant in the case claimed monetary damages for distress, anxiety, inconvenience, the cost of a new home and the expenses of moving house following the building and operation of a waste-treatment plant that had been situated next to her original home.[68] The Court accepted that 'Mrs López Ostra sustained some damage on account of the violation of Article 8. . . . Her old flat must have depreciated and the obligation to move must have entailed expense and inconvenience'. However, it was of the view that there was

> no reason to award her the cost of her new house since she [had] kept her former home [and that] [a]ccount must be taken of the fact that for a year the municipal authorities paid the rent of the flat occupied by the applicant and her family in the centre of Lorca and that the waste-treatment plant was temporarily closed by the investigating judge.[69]

The Court went on to award compensation for pecuniary and non-pecuniary damage suffered by the applicant, including from the gas fumes, noise and smells, as well as the anxiety and distress caused by the situation. As the heads of damage 'did not lend themselves to precise quantification', the Court awarded compensation on an equitable basis of ESP4 million.[70]

Many resolutions of the UN Human Rights Council have recognised the relationship between a healthy environment and the full realization of human rights.[71] A Special Rapporteur on human rights and the environment was appointed in 2015,[72] and in 2017 the Special Rapporteur warned in his annual report that pollution is one of the main causes of biodiversity degradation, which, in turn, hinders the full realization of human rights.[73] The Special Rapporteur concluded that

> [b]iodiversity is necessary for ecosystem services that support the full enjoyment of a wide range of human rights, including the rights to life, health, food, water and culture. In order to protect human rights, States have a general obligation to protect ecosystems and biodiversity.[74]

In the context of toxic dumping, the Human Rights Commission appointed a Special Rapporteur in 1995 with a mandate to investigate toxic dumping and its effects on human rights. The Special Rapporteur identified a number of human rights whose enjoyment is interfered with by toxic dumping.[75] It is evident, therefore, that dumping waste can have profound consequences, not just for the natural environment but also for human beings and the realisation of their fundamental rights.

International courts and tribunals as appropriate venues for environmental matters?

The cases explored previously raise the question of whether such tribunals are appropriate venues for the consideration of environmental matters. Cases involving environmental matters typically concern complex scientific issues, and, as is evident in the previous discussion, the disputes have come before tribunals that are not specialised in environmental law (although the ICJ has general jurisdiction). It has been said that international dispute settlement, particularly arbitration, has long been 'a means of delocalised, arms-length, and impartial dispute settlement for parties of different countries, opposing religious traditions, different systems and cultures of belief, among others who, in the ordinary course of circumstances, had no reason to trust the other'.[76] Indeed, international dispute settlement has over the years dealt with a wide variety of issues, from territorial delimitation, use of force, water rights and many others.[77] As such, we should not assume that tribunals are necessarily inappropriate venues for disputes involving complex environmental matters. But there are risks, such as the need to ensure that those tribunals without the requisite expertise to decide environmental protection cases properly engage with the matters at stake and do not dilute the law of environmental protection more generally. That said, this is a deficiency that could be remedied. In the recent jurisprudence I have discussed above, several promising signs are evident where tribunals have been called upon to adjudicate non-investment issues.

Some investment tribunals have shown signs that they are taking scientific matters seriously and have appointed their own experts to analyse scientific matters, as in *Perenco v. Ecuador* for example.[78] As alluded to earlier, the tribunal was aware of the complexity in appraising environmental damage and compensation. As a result, the tribunal appointed its own expert and allowed the parties' experts to comment on the reports of the tribunal-appointed expert, bolstering the transparency of the approach adopted by the tribunal.[79] In a different case, the *South China Sea Arbitration Between the Republic of the Philippines and the People's Republic of China*, a tribunal appointed its own *ex curia* experts. This was intended to give the tribunal its own 'independent opinion' on the environmental impact of the activities conducted by China in the South China Sea.[80]

However, there are also several legitimacy issues around the use of experts that remain to be addressed. In this context, international courts and tribunals will need to ensure they appropriately distinguish between matters of law and of science in drawing upon expertise.[81] The expert assists with determinations of fact and may be subject to certain procedural safeguards such as cross-examination or that the parties have the possibility to respond to and comment upon expertise provided by tribunal appointed experts, as was permitted in the *Perenco* case.

There are other entry points for expert or informed opinion on environmental matters. Tribunals may allow for the submission of *amicus curiae* briefs for example. Moreover, tribunals have sometimes looked to other judicial bodies or non-judicial institutions for the development of norms and interpretative guidance[82] and could similarly do so with specialised environmental institutions when they are faced with environmental matters.

Concluding remarks

An important aspect of the emerging practice on environmental compensation is the extent to which the assessments made by international courts and tribunals reflect a full picture of the environmental damage caused.[83] As such, the values of resources have been calculated by reference to techniques such as replacement cost, environmental services or value transfer approaches, among others. Unfortunately, some of these methods have significant blind spots and fail to account for environmental damage in its entirety, such as a diminution in carbon sequestration that can contribute to climate change.

One way to ameliorate these shortcomings would be to incorporate other values, such as non-use values, the intrinsic value of the ecosystem or equitable considerations in the calculation of environmental compensation, which may take into account a wider range of costs incurred. While such calculations are undoubtedly more complex, they are not impossible. Both international institutions and scholars have suggested possible approaches.[84] Moreover, as is evident from the previous exploration, human rights courts have valued non-pecuniary damages as well as incorporated equitable considerations in awarding compensation, including for environmental damage. More generally, techniques that recognise the broader costs in ecosystem services or egregious behaviour in grave environmental harm might better serve the preservation of resources and deter future environmentally risky behaviour. Further still, courts and tribunals should have recourse to experts, *amicus curiae* or other institutions to assist them in arriving at robust valuations of environmental damage.

As these kinds of cases come before international courts and tribunals more often, as is possible, it will be important to learn from the practice of other international regimes that have grappled with the appraisal of environmental compensation. We turn next to the practice of those regimes.

Notes

1 Draft Articles on Responsibility of States for Internationally Wrongful Acts with commentaries 2001, II(2) YBILC (2001), 101; see also *Trail Smelter Case (United States/Canada)*, III [1938 and 1941] Reports of International Arbitral Awards 1905, 1911.

2 *Certain Activities Carried Out By Nicaragua in the Border Area (Costa Rica v. Nicaragua) (Compensation)*, ICJ General List No. 150 (2 February 2018); *Burlington Resources v. Ecuador*, ICSID Case No. ARB/08/5, Decision on Ecuador's Counterclaim (7 February 2017); *Perenco v. Ecuador and Empresa Estatal Petróleos del Ecuador (Petroecuador)*, ICSID Case No. ARB/08/6, Interim Decision on the Environmental Counterclaim (11 August 2015).

3 The other two cases are the *Corfu Channel Case (Assessment of the Amount of Compensation Due from the People's Republic of Albania to the United Kingdom of Great Britain and Northern Ireland)* [1949] ICJ Rep 244 and *Case Concerning Ahmadou Sadio Diallo (Republic of Guinea v. Democratic Republic of the Congo)*, Compensation, Judgment [2012] ICJ Rep 324.

4 *Certain Activities Carried Out By Nicaragua in the Border Area (Costa Rica v. Nicaragua) – Compensation Owed by the Republic of Nicaragua to the Republic of Costa Rica*, ICJ General List No. 150 (2 February 2018), para 42.

5 *Certain Activities Carried Out By Nicaragua in the Border Area (Costa Rica v. Nicaragua)* and *Construction of a Road in Costa Rica along the San Juan River (Nicaragua v. Costa Rica)*, Judgment [2005] ICJ Rep 665.

6 Ibid., para 142.

7 *Costa Rica v. Nicaragua (Compensation)*.

8 Ibid., Memorial of Costa Rica, 26.

9 Ibid., para 52.

10 *Factory at Chorzów*, Jurisdiction [1927] PCIJ Series A, No. 9, 21 and *Factory at Chorzów*, Merits [1928] PCIJ Series A, No. 9, 47.

11 *Costa Rica v. Nicaragua (Compensation)*, para 86.

12 *Diallo*, op cit, para 33.

13 *Trail Smelter*, op cit.

14 *Story Parchment Company v. Paterson Parchment Paper Company* 282 [1931] United States Reports 555.

15 *Costa Rica v. Nicaragua (Compensation)*, para 35.

16 ICJ, 'Certain Activities Carried Out By Nicaragua in the Border Area (Costa Rica v. Nicaragua)–Question of Compensation–Nicaragua Transfers Total Amount of Compensation Awarded to Costa Rica', Press Release (23 March 2018).

17 *Costa Rica v. Nicaragua (Compensation)*, para 101.

18 Ibid., para 151.

19 Ibid.

20 Ibid., para 152.

21 *Diallo*, op cit, para 56.

22 *Costa Rica v. Nicaragua (Compensation)*, para 154.

23 *Chorzów Factory*, op cit, 47.

24 See, for example, *In the Matter of Oil Spill By the Amoco Cadiz Off the Coast of France on March 16, 1978*, 954 F. 2d 1279, 7th Cir. (1992).

25 *Costa Rica v. Nicaragua (Compensation)*, para 79.

26 Ibid., para 80.

27 Ibid., para 81.

28 *Maritime Delimitation in the Caribbean Sea and the Pacific Ocean (Costa Rica v. Nicaragua) / Land Boundary in the Northern Part of Isla Portillos (Costa Rica v. Nicaragua)*, ICJ General List Nos. 157 and 165 (2 February 2018).

29 *Pulp Mills on the River Uruguay (Argentina v. Uruguay)* [2010] ICJ Rep 14, particularly para 167.

30 Ibid., Dissenting Opinion: Judges Simma and Al-Khasawneh, paras 3 and 8.

31 *Whaling in the Antarctic (Australia v. Japan)* [2014] ICJ Rep 226, paras 74–5.

32 *Construction of a Road in Costa Rica along the San Juan River* (*Nicaragua v. Costa Rica*), Judgment (16 December 2015), paras 45, 175–6, 204.

33 *Maritime Delimitation in the Caribbean Sea and the Pacific Ocean (Costa Rica v. Nicaragua) / Land Boundary in the Northern Part of Isla Portillos (Costa Rica v. Nicaragua)*, General List Nos. 157 and 165 (2 February 2018), paras 14, 71, 73, and 86.

34 *Corfu Channel Case*, op cit; *Diallo*, op cit.

35 *Perenco Ecuador Ltd. v. The Republic of Ecuador and Empresa Estatal Petróleos del Eduador (Petroecuador)*, ICSID Case No. ARB/08/6, Interim Decision on the Environmental Counterclaim (11 August 2015).

36 Ibid., para 587.

37 *Burlington Resources Inc. v. Republic of Ecuador*, ICSID Case No. ARB/08/5.

38 *Costa Rica v. Nicaragua (Compensation)*, para 31.

39 See, for example, *I'm Alone Case*, III [1933–1935] Reports of International Arbitral Awards 1609; *Rainbow Warrior Affair*, XX [1990] Reports of International Arbitral Awards 215; *Eritrea-Ethiopia Claims Commission*, Final Award, 26 [2009] Reports of International Arbitral Awards 631, paras 103, 310–12.

40 Draft Articles on Responsibility of States for Internationally Wrongful Acts, Commentaries, op cit, 100; L'Institut de droit international, Final Report on Responsibility and Liability under International Law for Environmental Damage 1997, Annuaire de L'Institut de droit international (Pedone, 1996), 339.

41 *Costa Rica v. Nicaragua (Compensation)*, Dissenting Opinion: Judge *Ad Hoc* Dugard, paras 40–6.

42 See, for example, ibid.; *Perenco v. Ecuador*, op cit; *The Environment and Human Rights (State Obligations in Relation to the Environment in the Context of the Protection and Guarantee of the Rights to Life and to Personal Integrity: Interpretation and Scope of Articles 4(1) and 5(1) of the American Convention on Human Rights)*, IACtHR Advisory Opinion OC-23/17 of November 15, 2017. Series A No. 23; *Dispute Concerning Delimitation of the Maritime Boundary between Ghana and Cote d'Ivoire in the Atlantic Ocean (Ghana/Cote d'Ivoire)*, ITLOS Case No. 23 (23 September 2017). For a fuller exploration of trends and prospects in the extension of environmental protection through litigation, see Jason Rudall, *Altruism in International Law* (Cambridge University Press, forthcoming).

43 *Burlington Resources v. Ecuador*, op cit.

44 Ibid., para 18.

45 Ibid., para 34.

46 *Perenco v. Ecuador*, op cit.

47 Ibid., para. 587.

48 *Perenco v. Ecuador*, op cit.

49 *Burlington Resources v. Ecuador*, op cit, para 248.

50 *David Aven et al v. Costa Rica*, Award, DR-CAFTA Case No. UNCT/15/3 (18 September 2018).

51 Ibid., para 715.

52 Ibid., para 745.

53 Ibid., para 737.

54 Ibid., para 739.

55 See *Spyridon Roussalis v. Romania*, Award, ICSID Case No. ARB/06/1 (7 December 2011).

56 *Antoine Goetz & Consorts and SA Affinage des Metaux v. Burundi*, Award, ICSID Case No. ARB/01/2 (21 June 2012).

57 Eric de Brabandere, 'Human Rights and Foreign Direct Investment' in Markus Krajewski and Rhea Hoffmann (eds.), *Research Handbook on Foreign Direct Investment* (Edward Elgar, 2018).

58 *The Environment and Human Rights*, op cit.

59 Ibid.

60 Ibid.

61 Ibid., para 81.

62 Ibid., paras 81, 95 and 101.

63 Ibid., op cit.

64 Monica Feria-Tinta and Simon Milnes, 'The Rise of Environmental Law in International Dispute Resolution: Inter-American Court of Human Rights Issues Advisory Opinion on Environment and Human Rights' 27 (2016) *Yearbook of International Environmental Law* 64.

65 *Kaliña and Lokono Peoples v. Suriname* [2015] IACHR Series C, No. 309.
66 Ibid., para 290.
67 *López Ostra v. Spain*, Application No. 16798/90, A/303-C [1995] 20 EHRR 277.
68 Ibid., para 62.
69 Ibid., para 65.
70 Ibid.
71 See, for example, HRC Resolution 16/11 of 24 March 2011 on human rights and the environment; HRC Resolutions 7/23 of 28 March 2008, 10/4 of 25 March 2009 and 18/22 of 30 September 2011 on human rights and climate change; HRC Resolutions 9/1 of 24 September 2008 and 12/18 of 2 October 2009 on the adverse effects of the movement and dumping of toxic and dangerous products and wastes on the enjoyment of human rights and HRC Resolution 18/11 of 29 September 2011 on the mandate of the Special Rapporteur on the implications for human rights of the environmentally sound management and disposal of hazardous substances and wastes.
72 HRC Resolution 28/11 of 7 April 2015.
73 Report of the Special Rapporteur on the issue of human rights obligations relating to the enjoyment of a safe, clean, healthy and sustainable environment, 19 January 2017, UN Doc. A/HRC/34/49, 3.
74 Ibid., 21.
75 See also, Commission on Human Rights, Special Rapporteur to the UN Commission on Human Rights, *Adverse Effects of the Illicit Movement and Dumping of Toxic and Dangerous Products and Wastes on the Enjoyment of Human Rights* (21 December 2000), UN Doc. E/CN.4/2001/55/Add.1, para 58.
76 Diane Desierto, 'Why Arbitrate Business and Human Rights Disputes? Public Consultation Period Open for the Draft Hague Rules on Business and Human Rights Arbitration', *EJIL: Talk!*, 12 July 2019.
77 Ibid.
78 *Perenco v. Ecuador*, op cit.
79 Ibid., para 588.
80 *South China Sea Arbitration between the Republic of the Philippines and the People's Republic of China*, Award, PCA Case No. 2013–19, paras 84, 136 and 821.
81 Makane Moïse Mbengue, 'The Role of Experts before the International Court of Justice: The Whaling in the Antarctic Case' (2015) *Questions of International Law, Zoom-in* 14; Laurence Boisson de Chazournes, Makane Moïse Mbengue, Rukmini Das and Guillaume Gros, 'One Size Does Not Fit All – Uses of Experts before International Courts and Tribunals: An Insight into the Practice' 9(3) (2018) *Journal of International Dispute Settlement* 477.
82 See Jason Rudall, 'Not Just a Wit, But a Cause of Wit in Others: The Influence of Human Rights in International Litigation' in Avidan Kent, Nikos Skoutaris, and Jamie Trinidad (eds.), *The Future of International Courts: Regional, Institutional and Procedural Challenges* (Routledge, 2019); Ruti Teitel and Robert Howse, 'Cross-Judging: Tribunalization in a Fragmented But Interconnected Global Order' 41(1) (2008) *New York University Journal of International Law and Politics* 959, 989.
83 For example, in *Costa Rica v. Nicaragua (Compensation)* (ICJ ultimately adopted a market price approach, assigning market values to goods and services provided by the environment); *Burlington Resources v. Ecuador*, op cit (Tribunal applied strict liability remediation costs approach under Ecuadorian

domestic law); *Perenco v. Ecuador*, op cit (Tribunal appointed its own expert to value environmental damage under Ecuadorian law).

84 UNEP Working Group on Liability and Compensation for Environmental Damage arising from Military Activities, *Liability and Compensation for Environmental Damage* (UNEP, 1998), para 44; Michael Bowman, 'Biodiversity, Intrinsic Value, and the Definition and Valuation of Environmental Harm' in Michael Bowman and Alan Boyle (eds.), *Environmental Damage in International and Comparative Law: Problems of Definition and Valuation* (Oxford University Press, 2002); Freya Mathews, *The Ecological Self* (Routledge, 1991); Robin Attfield, *The Ethics of Environmental Concern* (2nd ed., University of Georgia Press, 1991).

3   International environmental compensation regimes

Introduction

This chapter zooms in on the practice of international regimes beyond international courts and tribunals to identify and assess other approaches for the valuation of environmental compensation. It similarly seeks to show how these regimes conceive of environmental damage, as well as tracing the broadening notion of such damage in certain regimes. Indeed, in this chapter we will examine the approaches of the United Nations Compensation Commission (UNCC), the International Oil Pollution Compensation (IOPC) regime, the frameworks governing liability for nuclear incidents, damage resulting from activities in space and Antarctica and deep seabed mining, as well as the Warsaw Mechanism for International Loss and Damage established to address the impacts of climate change. The chapter will also highlight the emergence of an ecosystems approach in conventions on the protection of the environment as well as other international institutional practice.

The United Nations Compensation Commission and environmental compensation

Following the 1990–1 Gulf War, UN Security Council resolution 687 (1991) created the UNCC, in the context of which claims for compensation of environmental damage were brought. Environmental claims were appraised by a specially constituted panel of Commissioners and were known as F4 claims. The Security Council resolution 'reaffirm[ed] that Iraq . . . is liable under international law for any direct loss, damage, including environmental damage and the depletion of natural resources . . . as a result of Iraq's unlawful invasion and occupation of Kuwait'.[1] While the Security Council found it difficult to define environmental damage,[2] the UNCC nevertheless endeavoured to do so. The UNCC had reviewed all 2.7 million claims by 2005, awarded USD52.4 billion to around 1.5 million successful claimants and USD48.7 billion in compensation claims has been paid out overall to date.[3] Around USD4.3 billion has been awarded by the UNCC to Iran, Jordan, Kuwait and Saudi Arabia for environmental remediation and restoration claims.[4] The experience of the UNCC can be valuable in shaping future approaches to environmental compensation.[5]

Affected States sought compensation for environmental damage. The Commissioners adjudicating upon the various claims were impartial experts and conducted their work independently from the UNCC Governing Council, which was a political body. They served in panels consisting of three members with each Commissioner on a panel being of a different nationality. The Panel reviewed written submissions produced by the various claimants, as well as the responses of Iraq at various stages of the process. Moreover, the Panel could ask for clarifications from the claimants and invite the submission of expert reports from consultants who were retained by the UNCC. The latter included reports from site visits. Further still, oral proceedings were held in which both the claimants and Iraq had a further opportunity to make submissions. The Commissioners then made findings of fact and of law and made recommendations as to awards of compensation to the UNCC Governing Council.[6]

Claims were required to be supported 'by documentary and other appropriate evidence sufficient to demonstrate the circumstances and amount of the claimed loss'.[7] Occasionally, this requirement was not met by claimants. For example, Turkey failed in its claim for damage to its forests due to the alleged impact of an influx of refugees. The Panel explained that it could not establish a causal link because Turkey had not supplied sufficient evidence such as 'the dates on which the refugees arrived in Turkey, the duration of their stay or the details of the damage that they are alleged to have caused'.[8]

The UNCC drew upon the advice of experts, information gathered from site visits, the submissions of the parties involved and responses to interrogatories that had been sent to claimants, as well as retaining legal and actuarial personnel of its own.[9] However, given the difficulties in the procedure, the Secretary of the Governing Council highlighted that 'the limited participation of the parties and particularly Iraq has resulted in the Commissioners and the Secretariat assuming an active investigative and fact-finding role in reviewing claims, with the assistance of outside expert consultants'.[10] In addition, the three commissioners dealing with environmental claims, namely Thomas Menash, Peter Sand and José Allen, were experts in international law, environmental damage and compensation for oil spills in particular.

During the submissions, the definition of environmental damage again proved to be controversial as different claimants adopted various definitions of this notion. Some claims focused on damage as physical or biological diminution while others claimed the possibility of contamination.[11] The F4 Panel ultimately adopted the approach that environmental damage means pollution that causes or is likely to cause physical or biological impairment or that leads to a reduction in utility by individuals.[12] This is also the approach taken under US law, as will become evident in the following chapter.

The damage caused by Iraq in its invasion of Kuwait included approximately 10.8 million barrels of oil by the Iraqi military in the sea and contaminated the coastline of Saudi Arabia,[13] around 6 million barrels of oil burning for almost 10 months,[14] over a billion barrels of oil released in Kuwait where Iraq exploded over 700 oil wells and contaminated groundwater and ecological systems,[15] damage caused by military activities, fortifications and mines left by Iraqi forces in Kuwait[16] and the movement of large numbers of refugees and their livestock through Iran, Jordan and Turkey, which damaged vegetation and water resources.[17] Compensation was claimed for the cleaning up of pollution, the restoration of ecosystems that had been damaged and the costs of monitoring public health and the environment.[18]

The UNCC appraised, valued and awarded compensation for the reparation of damaged soil, water, ecosystems and other environmental harm that resulted from Iraq's invasion of Kuwait. In doing so, it rejected Iraq's claim that pure environmental harm, that is harm to the environment having no commercial value and involving resources that could not be traded on the market, was not compensable. Iraq argued that the reference to 'financially assessable damage' in the ILC's Draft Articles meant any loss of resources that could not be traded on the market were not compensable as they could not be assessed in financial terms. The UNCC found that

> a loss due to depletion of or damage to natural resources, including resources that may not have a commercial value is, in principle, compensable in accordance with Security Council Resolution 687 (1991) and UNCC Governing Council decision 7 if such loss was a direct result of Iraq's invasion and occupation of Kuwait.[19]

Moreover, the UNCC was of the view that

> there is no justification for the contention that general international law precludes compensation for pure environmental damage. In particular, the Panel does not consider that the exclusion of compensation for pure environmental damage in some international conventions on civil liability and compensation is a valid basis for asserting that international

law, in general, prohibits compensation for such damage in all cases, even where the damage results from an internationally wrongful act.[20]

Indeed, as has been pointed out by Cymie R. Payne:

> Iraq's argument ignores the International Law Commission's further explanation that 'the qualification of "financially assessable" is intended to exclude compensation for . . . the affront or injury caused by a violation of rights not associated with actual damage to property or persons'.[21]

That said, the panel also cautioned that 'there are inherent difficulties in attempting to place a monetary value on damaged natural resources, particularly resources that are not traded in the market'.[22] It went on to refer to the *Trail Smelter* case in recognising the uncertainties in the valuation exercise for such resources:

> Where the [breach] itself is of such a nature as to preclude the ascertainment of the amount of damages with certainty, it would be a perversion of fundamental principles of justice to deny all relief to the injured person, and thereby relieve the wrongdoer from making any amend for his acts. In such case, while the damages may not be determined by mere speculation or guess, it will be enough if the evidence show the extent of the damages as a matter of just and reasonable inference, although the result be only approximate.[23]

The UNCC awarded compensation for a wide variety of environmental damage. For example, Kuwait had suffered damage to its shoreline and the UNCC awarded compensation for pure environmental damage in this context.[24] Compensation was granted to Jordan for damage to its groundwater resources as well as certain wildlife habitats.[25] Iran was compensated for rangeland damage that was the result of refugee camps.[26] Beyond compensation for pure environmental damage, the UNCC also awarded compensation for expenses and costs that resulted from the environmental damage, including for the abatement and prevention of environmental damage, measures taken to clean up and restore the damage, monitoring and assessment, public health screenings and the loss or damage of natural resources, as well as certain salaries of personnel.[27]

Security Council resolution 687 and UNCC Governing Council decision 7 envisaged 'direct' losses resulting from environmental harm could be the subject of an award. Moreover, the F4 Panel observed that 'expenses resulting from reasonable monitoring and assessment of loss or damage that may have occurred outside Iraq or Kuwait are, in principle, compensable'.[28] Some debate exists as to whether the commissioners dealing with environmental claims used a direct causation standard – which is generally a civil law standard – or at times utilised a proximate causation standard, which is generally a common law standard.[29] In the case of direct causation, no intervening event can break the causal chain whereas, in the case of proximate causation, proximately caused harm can be distinguished from harm that is too remote. It would seem that the panel used both approaches depending on the claim. In certain cases, intervening acts were held to break the chain of causation – for example where Kuwait had mismanaged the storage of retrieved ordnances originally left by Iraq but which spontaneously detonated – while in other cases Iraq's argument that the environmental damage resulting from the movement of refugees was not a direct consequence of the conflict was rejected by the panel, and it went on to award compensation to the claimant. This was the case in respect of Iran's claims for such damage when the panel found that there was sufficient 'evidence that the presence of the refugees resulted in environmental damage to rangeland areas [and] that this damage is a direct result [of the conflict]'.[30] That said, Jordan's claims that the movement of refugees had led to environmental damage in respect of water, agricultural lands, wetlands and marine life was rejected because of a failure to establish a causal link.[31]

It is interesting to note that the UNCC held Iraq liable for environmental damage even where there existed parallel and concurrent causes of damage. The panel made it clear that:

> Iraq is, of course, not liable for damage that was unrelated to its invasion and occupation of Kuwait nor for losses or expenses that are not a direct result of the invasion and occupation. However, Iraq is not exonerated from liability for loss or damage that resulted directly from the invasion and occupation simply because other factors might have contributed to the loss or damage. Whether or not any environmental damage or loss for which compensation is claimed was a direct result of Iraq's invasion and occupation of Kuwait will depend on the evidence presented in relation to each particular loss or damage.[32]

Compensation was mostly claimed for the costs incurred in responding to, monitoring, assessing, remediating and restoring the environmental damage. In certain circumstances, the remediation or restoration of environmental damage was not possible. This was the case, for example, where a shoreline ecosystem polluted by oil was too fragile to clean up manually. When it came to valuing such a case, the value of ecosystem services that had been lost was used.

Claims could generally be divided between those that concerned restoration costs – which was compensation sought for the reparation of the damaged resource or compensation for interim losses while the damaged resource was being repaired – and those that concerned compensation for the lost value of the damaged resources. Valuations were calculated using market- or non-market-based techniques. The restoration cost method was most often used. This values the compensation due by reference to the cost of repairing the damage. Such projects proposed by claimants had to be feasible and cost effective where several options were available, as well as offer a net benefit to the environment. In the alternative, certain compensation claims were calculated by having recourse to the loss in value of the resource. These were also calculated using market or non-market-based techniques, such as replacement costs approaches.

Often the cost of remediating the environmental damage was estimated, as was the case with the oil pollution damage to some of Saudi Arabia's coast.[33] In the particular circumstances of this case, remediation could not be conducted in the usual way given the fragility of the ecosystem affected. Instead, a slow natural process was used for the recovery of the area. This meant, however, that Saudi Arabia would lose ecosystem services for a longer period of time. In light of this, the F4 Panel used the habitat equivalency analysis (HEA) technique for valuing the amount of compensation it deemed most fair in these circumstances. This valuation technique accounts for the cost of replacement environmental projects intended to yield similar ecosystem services as the damaged resources. Applying the HEA valuation technique to Saudi Arabia's claim regarding its polluted shoreline, the Panel was of the view that two marine and coastal preserves could replace the outstanding ecosystem services and recommended that USD46.1 million be paid in compensation.[34] This HEA valuation technique was used in respect of other claims as well.[35]

We can learn many important lessons from the practice of the UNCC. First, the UNCC has been credited with instilling principles of environmental law into the practice of reparations, as well as utilizing advanced techniques for assessing environmental damage and establishing causation.[36] Second, the recourse made to technical expertise as the UNCC evaluated the environmental claims is notable.[37] Third, the UNCC Governing Council's guidelines and the practice of the F4 Panel help to define environmental damage and the types of losses or costs incurred therefrom, as well as illustrate the manifold approaches to assessing environmental compensation.[38] Fourth, traditionally State responsibility for environmental harm had been litigated in a bilateral way between a victim and an alleged wrongdoer, but the practice of the UNCC provides a blueprint for a multilateral mechanism that examines the legal accountability for environmental harm of many States involved in a given situation.[39]

With a view to improving upon the practice of the UNCC, several recommendations have been made by the consultants from Industrial Economics Incorporated (IEC), who provided scientific and technical expertise to the F4 claims panel. First, they have suggested establishing the definition of environmental damage as well as the acceptable methods for calculating compensation at the outset. Second, they note that data should be gathered as soon as possible after the environmental damage takes place to avoid the loss of perishable data. Third, they underlined the importance of site visits to inspect the environmental damage, meet with local experts and assess the most appropriate valuation techniques. Finally, they recommended maximising the transparency of the process. This is important for building confidence in the process and for all actors to learn from it.[40]

Several features of the UNCC process and approach are notable in the context of future environmental compensation assessment, particularly with climate change damage in mind. First, the UNCC decided to award compensation for damage to the environment that did not have a commercial value. Second, the adoption of a habitat equivalency analysis to calculate the value of lost ecosystem services by recourse to the cost of environmental projects intended to replace those ecosystem services. Third, remediation was defined by the Panel as the restoration of the environment to the conditions that existed prior to the invasion with respect to its general ecological state, rather than the remediation of specific incidents of environmental damage or pollution.[41] Fourth, the UNCC was concerned with the steps victims had taken to mitigate the damage after it had occurred. Fifth, compensation was awarded for the costs of monitoring or assessing environmental damage.[42] These are all pioneering and innovative approaches to valuing environmental damage for a quasi-judicial international body like the UNCC.

We now turn to consider another developed regime for environmental compensation at the international level. It has an institutional structure, as with the UNCC, although its approach differs in significant respects.

Compensation for oil pollution at sea

Following the Torrey Canyon oil spill of 1967, the international community was prompted to establish a framework for compensating those affected by oil spills. The International Convention on Civil Liability for Oil Pollution Damage (CLC) was initially adopted in 1969 and replaced in 1992 by a similar convention that revised the liability limits upwards.

The CLC provides for a regime that compensates those affected by oil pollution damage that results from oil spills from ships carrying oil in bulk. It allows for compensation to be claimed for the cost of reasonable measures taken after an incident to prevent or minimise damage caused by pollution. Moreover, the Convention makes the concerned ship owner liable for oil that has spilt. While there are exceptions, in principle liability is strict. That said, liability may be limited as regards any single incident so long as the owner has not been guilty of actual fault. Ship owners are required to have insurance for the amount equivalent to liability for one incident. The compensation limits, provided for in Special Drawing Rights (SDR) as used by the International Monetary Fund, are as follows: for a ship not exceeding 5,000 gross tonnage, liability is limited to 4.51 million SDR; for a ship between 5,000 to 140,000 gross tonnage, liability is limited to 4.51 million SDR plus 631 SDR for each additional gross tonne over 5,000; for a ship over 140,000 gross tonnage, liability is limited to 89.77 million SDR.

The CLC states in its preamble that it is intended to 'ensure that adequate compensation is available to persons who suffer damage caused by pollution resulting from the escape or discharge of oil from ships'. Adequate compensation is thus the standard of compensation adopted. This is potentially in tension with the liability limits set out by the CLC as described previously. However, a subsequent convention establishing a trust fund to make up for shortfalls was adopted and will be considered later.

Under the CLC, pollution damage is defined as

> loss or damage caused outside the ship by contamination from the escape or discharge of oil from the ship, wherever such escape or discharge may occur, provided that compensation for impairment of the environment other than loss of profit from such impairment shall be limited to costs of reasonable measures of reinstatement actually undertaken or to be undertaken [and] the costs of preventive measures and further loss or damage caused by preventive measures.[43]

At Article IX, the CLC provides that national courts should entertain and assess claims in accordance with the Convention. Several cases heard in national courts that concern the CLC will be considered in the next chapter.

In 1971, an International Convention on the Establishment of an International Fund for Compensation for Oil Pollution Damage created a fund (Fund 1971) that was intended to supplement the amount of compensation that could be obtained under the CLC. However, the amount of compensation needed for major spills had to be increased in two further conventions. These were the Civil Liability Convention 1992, replacing the CLC 1969 and the International Oil Pollution Compensation Fund 1992 (Fund 1992), replacing the Fund 1971. A protocol to the Fund 1992 known as the Supplementary Fund Protocol was adopted in 2003, which again extended the amount of compensation available under the Fund 1992. The International

Oil Pollution Compensation Funds (IOPC) are two inter-governmental organisations that administer the funds.

The funds are concerned with the liability and compensation for oil pollution caused by spills from oil tankers. Their Executive Assembly has issued guidance on evaluating environmental damage and calculating compensation.[44] They are replenished by contributions from various entities that may receive oil that has been transported across the sea. The different funds have dealt with 150 incidents since their establishment.[45]

Like the Fund 1971, the Fund 1992 is intended to supplement the CLC regime in an attempt to ensure full compensation is available for those affected by oil spills. Indeed, the Preamble of the Fund Convention 1992 provides that

> full compensation will be available to victims of oil pollution incidents and that the ship owners are at the same time given relief in respect of the additional financial burdens imposed on them.[46]

As such, where protection under the CLC is inadequate, the funds can make up for the difference between the amount owed by the ship owner and the cost of repairing the damage caused by the oil spill. Indeed, the funds pay compensation to those who may be affected from pollution damage but have been unable to receive full and adequate compensation under the CLC regime because no liability arises under the CLC, because the owner is financially incapable of providing compensation or because the amount needed to compensate the damage exceeds the limits prescribed under the CLC as outlined previously.

The funds' obligation to pay compensation is nevertheless limited to pollution that caused damage in the territories of Contracting States, including their territorial sea. That said, the funds must pay compensation to Contracting States in respect of any measures they take outside their territory. The funds also provide a possibility for Contracting States that may be threatened by pollution damage to receive financial assistance for measures they may take to prevent it. This can cover personnel, material, credit facilities or other aid.

For a compensation claim to be admissible, pollution damage must be quantifiable as an economic loss. This is shown by the claimant's production of accounting records or other evidence documenting such loss. Five types of pollution damage are identified by the IOPC: (1) property damage; (2) costs of clean-up operations at sea and on shore; (3) economic losses by fishermen or those engaged in mariculture; (4) economic losses in the tourism sector; and (5) costs for reinstatement of the environment.[47] Compensation may be awarded for reasonable reinstatement measures designed to speed up the natural recovery of environmental damage, although compensation for interim losses is not permitted.[48] Claims that concern non-market valuations are not compensable. This includes, for example, stated preference valuation techniques like contingent valuation, travel costs, habitat or resource equivalency analyses, hedonic pricing or benefits transfer approaches.[49]

Claimants may include individuals, partnerships, companies, private organisations or public bodies, such as States or local authorities. Experts are generally appointed by the fund to assess the losses, to monitor clean-up operations and to evaluate the technical aspects of a given claim.[50] However, the IOPC has been criticised for the vague nature of the definition of pollution damage under the CLC and Fund frameworks. The IOPC has been resistant to clarifying or extending the notion of pollution damage because of a fear that this might lead to an influx of expensive pure environmental damage claims.[51]

A 1979 incident involving the oil spill from the vessel *Antonio Gramsci* led to the Soviet Union submitting a claim for GBP43 million to the IOPC Funds. It illustrates the reluctance of the IOPC Funds to change their prescribed methods for environmental compensation assessment. In the case, the Soviet Union claimed the amount for damage to the marine environment and to compensate expenses incurred from the purification of the polluted waters. The State had estimated the pollution cost based on a mathematical model known as *methodika*, which estimates total pollution according to units of seawater that have been polluted. However, the IOPC rejected the claim and confirmed that mathematical models could not be used to quantify pollution damage. A resolution adopted by the IOPC Assembly subsequently provided that 'the assessment of compensation to be paid by the IOPC fund is not to be made on the basis of an abstract quantification of damage calculated in accordance with theoretical models'.[52] That said, reinstatement measures can now be compensated, but these are appraised by the IOPC as described previously.

The model of the IOPC Funds is also apparent in other regimes governing liability for dangerous activities. We now turn to that concerning compensation for nuclear incidents.

Compensation for nuclear incidents

The Convention on Third Party Liability in the Field of Nuclear Energy of 1960, which has since been amended by the Additional Protocol of 1964 and the Protocol of 1982, provides for compensation in respect of nuclear incidents. The Convention aims in its preamble to ensure that compensation should be 'adequate and equitable' for those who are victims of damage caused by nuclear incidents. Article 3 establishes the liability of the operator of a nuclear installation for damage or loss of life and damage to or loss of property resulting from a nuclear incident. The definition of nuclear incidents under the Convention give an insight into the environmental damage that is envisaged. As such, a nuclear incident includes:

> any occurrence or succession of occurrences having the same origin which causes damage, provided that such occurrence or succession of occurrences, or any of the damage caused, arises out of or results either from the radioactive properties, or a combination of radioactive properties with toxic, explosive, or other hazardous properties of nuclear fuel or radioactive products or waste or with any of them, or from ionizing radiations emitted by any source of radiation inside a nuclear installation.[53]

Article 11 provides that '[t]he nature, form and extent of the compensation, within the limits of this Convention, as well as the equitable distribution thereof, shall be governed by national law', while Article 13 provides that jurisdiction for the determination of claims lies with the courts in the Contracting Party where the incident happened or in the courts of the Contracting Party where the nuclear installation of the operator liable is situated if the incident occurred outside the territory of a Contracting Party. The amount of compensation and period during which compensation may be claimed is limited. We will explore these features in more detail.

As a result of this Convention regime, the operator of a nuclear installation is held to be exclusively liable for any damage that results from a nuclear incident. Indeed, it is the operator of a nuclear installation where the nuclear incident occurs who must be held liable. Alternatively, where an incident occurs while nuclear material is being shipped, the operator of the installation from where the material came from is liable. The reason for such an exclusive liability regime is twofold, and this exclusivity is distinct from the approach taken in other legal systems with respect to tortious liability. First, the approach under the Convention regime simplifies the process of apportioning liability. It avoids complicated litigation to determine who is individually liable for what action. Second, the approach only renders it necessary for the operator to take out insurance. Those who may be affiliated with the nuclear installation do not necessarily need separate insurance cover for damage caused.[54]

A further feature of this regime is that it imposes strict liability on the operator. While a presumption of liability usually attaches to dangerous activities in many legal systems, this Convention regime goes a step further and removes all fault assessments. Given the extraordinarily hazardous nature of nuclear activities, as well as the complexities involved in determining fault or negligence in such a context, strict liability was the approach adopted.

It is also important to highlight that exclusive jurisdiction is granted to the courts of a State. This means that courts in other States cannot entertain litigation concerning the Convention. The courts of the Contracting Party where the nuclear incident happened have jurisdiction. This solves the problem of multiple proceedings involving different awards of compensation in various jurisdictions. Whichever courts are seized of the litigation can hear claims concerning the operator, insurers or other guarantors as regards compensation arising from the nuclear incident connected with a nuclear installation in that country.

The Convention regime also limits liability in quantum and time. These circumscribe the amount an operator may be obliged to pay out as a result of a nuclear incident. If such restrictions did not exist, it is more likely that the operator would not have the financial resources to meet claims and also may not be able to obtain insurance.[55] Moreover, the operator may not be in a position to retain significant sums in reserve in case claims are made long after an incident. That said, it is also important to highlight that injury to human beings resulting from radioactive material may only become evident after a long period of time has elapsed. A balance has thus had to be achieved between these two competing interests described.

A similar regime is established by the Vienna Convention on Civil Liability for Nuclear Damage of 1963. While a minimum amount of compensation is set by the Vienna Convention, unlike the Convention on Third Party Liability in the Field of Nuclear Energy 1960, a maximum amount is not (although this may be provided for by Contracting Parties). Once again, under this regime, national courts are empowered to determine the amounts of compensation due. The 1997 Protocol to the Vienna Convention (1997 Protocol) stipulates that compensation should be 'adequate and equitable' in its preamble and prioritises compensation claims that concern loss of life or personal injury.[56] A further Convention on Supplementary Compensation for Nuclear Damage 1997 (CSC 1997) establishes a framework for nuclear and non-nuclear States. Both 1997 instruments raised the amounts of compensation available, as well as broadening the scope of damage covered and the jurisdiction envisaged. We will explore these developments in more detail now.

Under the 1997 Protocol and the CSC 1997, 300 million SDR is the minimum amount a State must make available for the compensation of nuclear damage. This amount is much higher than the minimum amounts required by the previous conventions on nuclear liability. Moreover, the CSC 1997 establishes an international fund that is intended to supplement any compensation that may be claimed from the operator. The fund is mainly replenished by nuclear power generating States, while contributions from other States are also solicited based on their United Nations rates of assessment. Half of the international fund exclusively covers transboundary damage.[57]

The definition of 'nuclear damage' is broadened under the 1997 regime as it identifies and expands the specific kinds of damage that should be compensated. The definition includes personal injury and property damage, which was also provided for in the existing definition. However, the new definition also includes a number of categories of damage that are concerned with the impairment of the environment, preventive measures and economic loss. These categories are thus compensable under national law and by a domestic court. It is now clear that environmental damage caused by a nuclear incident is compensable under the regime, as are preventive measures taken and certain economic loss.

The definition of 'nuclear incident' is also revised by the 1997 regime. As such, even where radiation has not been released, preventive measures can be taken to avoid a grave and imminent threat of a release of radiation. The reference to 'grave and imminent' implies that preventive measures can be taken where there is a credible basis for suspecting that radiation may be released. Such preventive measures must be reasonable, as must measures of reinstatement relating to impairment of the environment.

As is becoming evident, there are a number of common features in the previous liability regimes. Some of these features are also present in the regime on liability for activities conducted in space, to which we now turn.

Compensation under the Space Liability Convention

The Convention on International Liability for Damage Caused by Space Objects of 1972 (Space Liability Convention) places absolute liability on States that launch or procure the launching of a space object – or on States whose territory has been used for the launch of a space object – for damage caused to the earth or to aircraft. Under the Space Liability Convention, damage is defined as the loss of life, personal injury or impairment of health or loss of or damage to property. The principle of full compensation is provided for under Article XII, which sets out:

> The compensation which the launching State shall be liable to pay for damage under this Convention shall be determined in accordance with international law and the principles of justice and equity, in order to provide such reparation in respect of the damage as will restore the person, natural or juridical, State or international organisation on whose behalf the claim is presented to the condition which would have existed if the damage had not occurred.

Interestingly, where a claim cannot be settled through diplomatic means, as is set out under Article IX, Article XIV provides that a Claims Commission may be established. The Claims Commission can decide on both the merits of any claim and the amount of compensation that must be paid. The Space Liability Convention does not set liability limits, as is the case in the IOPC regime, for example. It is an absolute liability regime.

One well-known case gives an insight into the regime. In an incident known as the *Cosmos* case,[58] a Soviet satellite named *Cosmos 954* disintegrated and scattered partly radioactive material over Canadian territory in 1978. Canada claimed compensation for the costs it incurred locating the satellite, as well as retrieving it, testing the radioactive materials and cleaning up the affected areas.

A claims commission was not set up in the *Cosmos* case, and it was ultimately settled through diplomatic channels. Canada asserted that it had calculated the compensation it claimed it was owed by reference to

> the relevant criteria established by general principles of international law according to which fair compensation is to be paid, by including in its claim only those costs that are reasonable, proximately caused by the intrusion of the satellite and deposit of debris and capable of being calculated with a reasonable degree of certainty.[59]

The impact of the satellite did not cause any damage upon impact, but the radioactive elements meant the clean-up operation had to be conducted with great care given the risk to human life and the environment presented by the presence of radioactive material. It cost Canada CAD13,970,143.66 to locate, remove and clean up the affected area. Canada mostly relied on general principles of international law in its claim for damage to the environment, as environmental damage is not expressly provided for under the 1972 Convention, although it also argued that damage to property covered by the Convention should extend to clean-up, reparation and prevention activities.[60] While it claimed almost double, in 1981 the Soviet Union ultimately paid CAD3 million in compensation but did not admit responsibility for any wrongdoing.

It is important to note that the approach claimed by Canada was later reflected in a resolution adopted by the UN General Assembly in 1992 entitled 'Principles Relevant to the Use of Nuclear Power Sources in Outer Space'.[61] In particular, Principle 9 is concerned with liability and compensation. It provides that compensation includes 'reimbursement of the duly substantiated expenses for search, recovery and clean-up operations, including expenses for assistance received from third parties'.[62] This would, in turn, appear to confirm that damage under the Space Liability Convention can include that to the natural environment, and reparation of such environmental damage can be compensated.[63]

In the alternative, a regime that specifically provides for environmental damage, including damage to biodiversity, species, fauna and flora as well as the marine environment, climate and the air is that applying to activities in Antarctica. We turn to consider that regime in the next section.

Liability for environmental damage in Antarctica

The 1991 Protocol on Environmental Protection to the Antarctic Treaty is intended to protect the environment of the Antarctic, but it is also concerned with protecting 'dependent and associated ecosystems and the intrinsic value of Antarctica, including its wilderness and aesthetic values'. It defines adverse effects broadly in its Article 3, including those on biological diversity, endangered species, fauna and flora, marine and terrestrial environments, climate and weather as well as the quality of the air and water. Article 7 bans any mining of mineral resources in Antarctica, and Article 16 envisages the imposition of liability for activities that cause damage. Annex VI is entitled Liability Arising from Environmental Emergencies and was adopted by the Antarctic Treaty Consultative Meeting in 2005, after 13 years of discussions on this so-called liability annex to the Antarctica Protocol.[64] That said, it is not yet in force. An environmental emergency is defined under the Annex in Article 2 as 'any accidental event that has occurred . . . and that results in, or imminently threatens to result in, any significant and harmful impact on the Antarctic environment'. It goes on to require operators to take response action to environmental emergencies in Article 5. Operators responsible for damage who fail to take action to remedy the damage are liable to pay compensation for the cost of reparation action taken by any of the parties. Liability is strict.

Article 6 provides, among other elements, for the liability of operators who fail to take prompt and effective response actions where environmental emergencies occur that result from the activities of the operator. The operator is liable for the costs of the response action that should have been undertaken. That said, Article 9 provides for limitations on the amount of liability an operator may be held liable for:

1   The maximum amount for which each operator may be liable under Article 6(1) or Article 6(2), in respect of each environmental emergency, shall be as follows:

    (a) for an environmental emergency arising from an event involving a ship:

        (i) one million SDR for a ship with a tonnage not exceeding 2,000 tons;

    (ii) for a ship with a tonnage in excess thereof, the following amount in addition to that referred to in (i) above:

- for each ton from 2,001 to 30,000 tons, 400 SDR;
- for each ton from 30,001 to 70,000 tons, 300 SDR; and
- for each ton in excess of 70,000 tons, 200 SDR;

(b) for an environmental emergency arising from an event which does not involve a ship, three million SDR.

Where the environmental emergency results from reckless or intentionally wrongful behaviour, liability is not limited.

Another regime that governs an area beyond national jurisdiction is that concerning the law of the sea. In that context, the Area is defined as 'the seabed and ocean floor and subsoil thereof, beyond the limits of national jurisdiction'.[65] We consider the emphasis placed on environmental protection, particularly with respect to mining activities in the deep sea bed, under that regime next.

Liability and deep seabed mining

The 1982 UN Convention on the Law of the Sea (UNCLOS) provides for various obligations to protect the marine environment.[66] This includes the protection and preservation of the ecological balance, marine flora and fauna, as well as certain ecosystems, habitats and marine life. Article 1(4) defines pollution as the introduction of substances that can result in harm to living resources and marine life.

Part XI of UNCLOS regulates mining in the Area. In this context, the International Seabed Authority (ISA) was established and regulations on the mining of polymetallic nodules were developed. The regulations provide for liability and compensation. States may be liable for damage caused by their nationals who carry out mining activities only if those States fail in their responsibilities as spelt out under Article 139 of Part XI UNCLOS. The responsibility and liability of contractors who conduct operations in the Area is provided for in Article 22 of Annex III to the Convention. As such, a contractor is liable 'for the actual amount of any damage arising out of wrongful acts in the conduct of its operations'. Article 145 UNCLOS provides for the protection of the Area when activities are being conducted there. It empowers the ISA to adopt rules to ensure 'the prevention, reduction and control of pollution and other hazards to the marine environment' as well as 'the protection and conservation of the natural resources of the Area and the prevention of damage to the flora and fauna of the marine environment'.

The Regulations on Prospecting and Exploration for Polymetallic Nodules in the Area were developed and approved by the ISA.[67] They place an emphasis on environmental protection. For example, they prevent the undertaking of prospecting activities where such activities present a risk of 'serious harm to the marine environment'. Regulation 1 defines 'serious harm to the marine environment'. The 'marine environment' includes

the physical, chemical, geological and biological components, conditions and factors which interact and determine the productivity of, state, condition and quality of the marine ecosystem, the waters of the seas and oceans and the airspace above those waters, as well as the seabed and ocean floor and subsoil thereof.

'Serious harm' is then defined as

any effect from activities in the Area on the marine environment which represents a significant adverse change in the marine environment determined according to the rules, regulations and procedures adopted by the Authority on the basis of internationally recognised standards and practices.

This definition does not mention restoration or reinstatement of the environment, and it is not clear whether a contractor would be liable to pay both the costs of preventative measures as well as that of any damage actually incurred.[68] That said, full reinstatement of the environment on the deep seabed may be difficult if not impossible.

Any prospecting activity that does take place must be conducted in accordance with the rules and regulations for marine environment protection as provided for by the ISA. Part V of the Regulations is concerned with the Protection and Preservation of the Marine Environment. It provides for strict obligations for the contractor engaged in prospecting activities in the Area as well as for the ISA. The Secretary-General of the ISA must be notified of any serious harm to the environment. Moreover, where this occurs the contractor is obliged to take emergency measures. The Secretary-General may also order emergency measures in the event of a serious incident and recover the costs of such measures from the contractor.

The Standard Clauses for Exploration Contracts in this context also squarely place liability and the cost of any damage on the contractor. Indeed, paragraph 16.1 sets out that '[t]he Contractor shall be liable for the actual amount of any damage, including damage to the marine environment, arising out of its wrongful acts or omissions'.[69]

We turn now to a relatively new approach for compensating damage to the environment. It is one that does not seek to attribute liability but rather simply provides common pecuniary relief for loss and damage that results from climate change.

Loss and damage in the climate change regime

The Warsaw International Mechanism for Loss and Damage associated with Climate Change Impacts is a non-contentious approach to repairing damage caused by climate change. This mechanism came into being at the 19th Conference of the Parties (COP) of the UN Framework Convention on Climate Change (UNFCCC) and was incorporated in the Paris Agreement at COP 21.[70] It does not seek to repair past damage nor attribute liability.[71] Rather, the Warsaw Mechanism is future facing and communitarian. It is intended to address future risks associated with climate change and offer the necessary financial resources. The Paris Agreement of 2015 recognises in its Article 8 'the importance of averting, minimizing and addressing loss and damage associated with the adverse effects of climate change, including extreme weather events and slow onset events, and the role of sustainable development in reducing the risk of loss and damage'. It goes on to provide that:

4   Accordingly, areas of cooperation and facilitation to enhance understanding, action and support may include:

    a)   Early warning systems;
    b)   Emergency preparedness;
    c)   Slow onset events;
    d)   Events that may involve irreversible and permanent loss and damage;
    e)   Comprehensive risk assessment and management;
    f)   Risk insurance facilities, climate risk pooling and other insurance solutions;
    g)   Non-economic losses; and
    h)   Resilience of communities, livelihoods and ecosystems.

The present day legal principle of loss and damage has developed from a political concept that first emerged in the 1990s when small island States sought to secure compensation and insurance within the rubric of the UNFCCC to cover losses resulting from sea level rises.[72] As the effects of climate change became apparent and scientific understanding crystallised, the importance of loss and damage in climate discussions became evident.

An open question in the climate change regime generally is whether States who emit large amounts of greenhouse gases can be held liable for damage that climate change causes to vulnerable States. The decision that adopts the Paris Agreement provides that Article 8 on loss and damage 'does not involve or provide a basis for any liability or compensation'.[73] However, when ratifying the Paris Agreement a number of Pacific Island States issued a declaration that their acceptance

> shall in no way constitute a renunciation of any rights under international law concerning State responsibility for the adverse effects of climate change and that no provision in the Paris Agreement can be interpreted as derogating from principles of general international law or any claims or rights concerning compensation due to the impacts of climate change.[74]

In particular, international courts could contribute to rendering justice for small island States, developing countries and other countries that have contributed little to global greenhouse emissions but are likely to be most severely affected by the consequences of climate change.[75] However, it remains to be seen whether such a case will come before an international court or tribunal.

In appraising loss and damage, it is important to recognise that significant intangible harm is likely to result from climate change, in addition to tangible economic harm. This will bring into sharp focus the importance of techniques of valuation that reflect non-economic, inherent or intrinsic value. Climate-related harm is likely to result from floods, droughts, increased temperature and heat waves, storms, sea level rises, glacial melting and reduced sea ice, as well as bush, forest and wildfires.[76] As for intangible values potentially affected by climate change, a recent study has indicated the following: culture, lifestyle, traditions and heritage; physical health; mental and emotional wellbeing; human mobility; indirect economic benefits and opportunities; sense of place; ecosystem services; social fabric; biodiversity and species; knowledge and ways of knowing; productive land; human life; identity; habitat; self-determination and influence; order in the world; dignity; territory; ability to solve problems collectively; and sovereignty.[77] Indeed, this comprehensive study of intangible climate-related harm has cautioned that much research conducted to date significantly underestimates the amount of non-economic loss and damage for those living in poverty or low-income countries.[78] Moreover, it has been observed that 'existing technical and quantitative assessment methodologies overlook or are ill equipped to capture many of the intangible values people consider important and subject to climate-related harm'.[79]

Other international practice has defined environmental harm in relation to compensation regimes more clearly and often with a broader conception of such harm. We will consider a few examples of these next.

Other international practice on compensation for environmental damage

Several other major international conventions and soft law instruments address environmental compensation. On 5 March 2018, for example, the Nagoya-Kuala Lumpur Supplementary Protocol on Liability and Redress to the Cartagena Protocol on Biosafety in the context of the Convention on Biodiversity of 1992 entered into force. It provides international rules and procedures on liability and redress with respect to living modified organisms. In particular, it requires the taking of response measures where damage occurs that has resulted from living modified organisms. Damage is defined under Article 2 of the Protocol as

> an adverse effect on the conservation and sustainable use of biological diversity, taking also into account risks to human health, that:
>
> i   Is measurable or otherwise observable taking into account, wherever available, scientifically-established baselines recognized by a competent authority that takes into account any other human induced variation and natural variation; and
> ii Is significant as set out in paragraph 3 below.

A significant adverse effect is also defined under the same provision as being determined on the basis of such factors as (i) a change that is long-term or permanent, such that it does not recover naturally in a reasonable period of time; (ii) an extensive change in terms of quality or quantity that affects biological diversity; (iii) a reduced ability of elements of biological diversity to deliver goods and services; (iv) the extent of adverse impacts on human health.

As for the response measures that are expected under Article 2 of the Protocol, these can include reasonable actions to:

i   Prevent, minimize, contain, mitigate, or otherwise avoid damage, as appropriate;
ii Restore biological diversity through actions to be undertaken in the following order of preference:

> a   Restoration of biological diversity to the condition that existed before the damage occurred, or its nearest equivalent; and where the competent authority determines this is not possible;
> b   Restoration by, inter alia, replacing the loss of biological diversity with other components of biological diversity for the same, or for another type of use either at the same or, as appropriate, at an alternative location.

The 1999 Protocol on Liability and Compensation for Damage resulting from Transboundary Movements of Hazardous Wastes and their Disposal to the 1989 Basel Convention on the Control of Transboundary Movements of Hazardous Wastes and their Disposal similarly addresses the form of environmental damage and provides for financial responsibility where an incident occurs. All of the phases of the transboundary movement of wastes, from loading to transportation means, to export, import and final disposal are addressed by the Protocol. It develops a definition of damage in Article 2(c) as meaning:

> (i) Loss of life or personal injury; (ii) Loss of or damage to property other than property held by the person liable in accordance with the present Protocol; (iii) Loss of income directly deriving from an economic interest in any use of the environment, incurred as a result of impairment of the environment, taking into account savings and costs; (iv) The costs of measures of reinstatement of the impaired environment, limited to the costs of measures actually taken or to be undertaken; and (v) The costs of preventive measures, including any loss or damage caused by such measures, to the extent that the damage arises out of or results from hazardous properties of the wastes involved in the transboundary movement and disposal of hazardous wastes and other wastes subject to the Convention.

Furthermore, under Article 2(d) and (e) of the Protocol, measures of reinstatement are defined as 'any reasonable measures aiming to assess, reinstate or restore damaged or destroyed components of the environment', while preventive measures mean 'any reasonable measures taken by any person in response to an incident, to prevent, minimize, or mitigate loss or damage, or to effect environmental clean-up'.

It has been observed that this provides a much clearer definition of damage and the consequences and actions that should follow such damage than that under the IOPC framework, for example.[80] This is largely achieved by the way in which the various heads of damage are set out separately and each is defined. Moreover, measures of reinstatement create a positive duty of restoration, and an explicit reference to the costs of assessing the damage is made. Finally, the Protocol goes further in the direction of compensating pure environmental damage.

Other international organisations, commissions and instruments are also of note for their practice on environmental compensation. For example, the Principles on the Allocation of Loss in the Case of Transboundary Harm Arising Out of Hazardous Activities were drafted by the ILC and were taken note of by the General Assembly of the UN in Resolution 61/36 of

4 December 2006. The instrument provides in its Preamble that 'appropriate and effective measures should be in place to ensure that those natural and legal persons, including States, that incur harm and loss as a result of such incidents are able to obtain prompt and adequate compensation'.

Another example is the methodologies for the calculation of environmental compensation developed by UN Environment.[81] It suggested that a range of environmental costs should be taken into account, not just those directly resulting from a clean-up operation.[82] Moreover, the UN Environment Programme has issued Guidelines for the Development of Domestic Legislation on Liability, Response Action and Compensation for Damage Caused by Activities Dangerous to the Environment in 2010.[83]

Similarly, UN Environment Programme's Manual on Compliance with and Enforcement of MEAs lists a number of criteria to be taken into account in determining monetary penalties. These include: (1) the economic benefit from delayed compliance; (2) the nature, extent and gravity of the violation; (3) the degree of the violator's culpability or wilfulness; (4) the extent of the violator's good faith efforts to comply; (5) the history of prior violations; (6) the economic impact of the penalty on the violator; (7) the deterrent effect of the penalty; (8) the costs incurred by the State as a result of the violation and (9) other relevant factors.[84] This would suggest that the behaviour of parties should be taken into account in the appraisal of compensation. However, it is important to remember that punitive or exemplary damages are not yet accepted under international law, as discussed earlier.

Further still, in 1997 the Ramsar Convention Secretariat published a guide for policymakers and planners on the monetary valuation of wetlands. The valuation framework recommended was the total economic value formula, which we will consider in Chapter 5, and it includes both direct use values as well as indirect use values such as losses resulting from intangible harm. It also develops a cost-benefit analysis technique to value the environmental functions served by a wetland.[85]

The *Institut de droit international* (IDI) has similarly addressed the issues of liability for environmental damage under international law. The IDI is composed of particularly influential lawyers who have had an impact on the development of environmental law, as well as other areas such as the law of armed conflict or regulation concerning the seabed and outer space.[86] Indeed, Article 1(2) of its Statutes provides that the purpose of the IDI is to 'promote the progress of international law'. Since its foundation – and despite the fact that it lacks any official nature – the IDI has been perceived as an important authority on international law and has had a profound impact on the rules of international law.

In a resolution of 1997 concerned with 'Responsibility and Liability under International Law for Environmental Damage', the IDI distinguished between pure environmental damage and damage to life or property.[87]

Indeed, Article 23 of the resolution provides that regimes should provide for the reparation of environmental damage as such. This should be distinct from the reparation of damage concerning death, personal injury or loss of property or economic value, which can also be provided for separately.

In Article 24, the resolution encourages the provision of a broad concept of reparation. Reparation should include the cessation of the concerned action, restitution, compensation and satisfaction where appropriate. Compensation must include the costs of repairing the environment as well as other economic loss. The resolution notes that environmental regimes could also provide for compensation that is appraised on the basis of equitable considerations as well as criteria developed in international conventions and by the judiciary. That equitable considerations may be factored into an assessment of compensation provides a margin of discretion for courts to have regard for such matters as the need to protect and conserve the environment, the importance of measures in the fight against climate change and the behaviour of the parties in a case. This was the view of dissenting Judge Ad Hoc Dugard in the *Costa Rica v. Nicaragua* case concerning compensation, as discussed in the previous chapter.[88]

Article 25 stipulates that irreparable or unquantifiable environmental damage should not be exempt from compensation. It explains that the contrary could result in an entity paying less in compensation where more serious environmental harm is inflicted. Instead, the resolution encourages the development of criteria for the assessment of damage that is irreparable for physical, technical or economic reasons. It even goes on to suggest categories of non-tangible damage that could be compensated in environmental regimes, such as the impairment of use, aesthetic and other non-use values, intergenerational equity and generally equitable assessment. That said, the provision also cautions that full reparation of environmental damage should not amount to excessive, exemplary or punitive compensation being awarded, although the IDI has also urged in another context that 'where it would be equitable for compensation to exceed actual loss or some other alternative measurement punitive damages might be envisaged. Deliberate environmental damage might be a case in point'.[89]

The resolution of the IDI suggests that a wider range of factors should inform the assessment of compensation and, moreover, that environmental harm be conceived in a broader sense. The latter is also increasingly reflected in environmental conventions, to which we now turn.

Broadening notions of environmental harm

Conceptions of environmental harm may differ from treaty to treaty. That said, an increasing number of treaties define such harm in broad terms, recognising the intrinsic connections in the natural environment. This is particularly evident with the emergence of an ecosystems approach. Understandings of environmental harm are generally not limited to the loss of resources having economic value to human beings. Indeed, harm can include the intrinsic value of ecosystems and biological diversity, for example. Many different regimes have defined the environment as including the air, water, soil, fauna, flora, ecosystems and the interaction of ecosystems, as well as amenity, cultural heritage and landscape.[90] In fact, the ILC's Commentary to the Draft Articles on State Responsibility notes that

> environmental damage will often extend beyond that which can be readily quantified in terms of clean-up costs or property devaluation. Damage to such environmental values (bio-diversity, amenity, etc, sometimes referred to as 'non-use values') is, as a matter of principle, no less real and quantifiable than damage to property, though it may be difficult to quantify.[91]

In 1998, a Working Group of Experts on Liability and Compensation for Environmental Damage defined such damage as a 'change that has a measurable adverse impact on the quality of a particular environment or any of its components, including its use and non-use values, and its ability to support and sustain an acceptable quality of life and a viable ecological balance'.[92] The 2009 'UNEP Draft Guidelines for the development of national legislation on liability, response action and compensation for damage caused by activities dangerous to the environment' define environmental damage in a more detailed way, providing that it includes:

> an adverse or negative effect on the environment that: (a) Is measurable taking into account scientifically established baselines recognised by a public authority that takes into account other human-induced variation and natural variation; and (b) Is significant which is to be determined on the basis of factors, such as: (i) The long term or permanent change, to be understood as change that will not be redressed through natural recovery within a reasonable period of time; (ii) The extent of the qualitative or quantitative changes that adversely or negatively affect the environment; (iii) The reduction or loss of the ability of the environment to provide goods and services wither of a permanent nature or of a temporary basis; (iv) The extent of any adverse or negative effect/ impact on human health; (v) The aesthetic, scientific, and recreational value of parks, wilderness areas, and other lands.[93]

Several treaty regimes adopt an ecosystems approach. An ecosystems approach requires States to protect both land and water resources from degradation, such as by reducing deforestation and overgrazing or controlling pollution of these resources.[94] The approach recognises the many threats to the integrity of an ecosystem and in this way encourages a comprehensive approach to protecting and preserving the ecosystem. It demands a consideration of entire systems of living resources interconnected with their natural environment, as well as the way in which human activity affects them.[95]

While an ecosystem approach is not yet a requirement of customary international law, it is increasingly evident in international environmental law.[96] The approach is apparent in the Convention on the Ozone Layer 1985, UNFCCC 1992, the Convention on Wetlands of International Importance Especially as Waterfowl Habitat 1975,[97] the Great Lakes Water Quality Agreement 1978, the UNECE Water Convention 1992 and the Mekong Agreement 1995, in the 2008 Draft Articles on Transboundary Aquifers and the UNECE Model Rules on Transboundary Groundwaters, for example. Moreover, an ecosystem approach was a critical element of the 1992 Convention on Biological Diversity (CBD), and it is evident from the fifth meeting of the CoP of the CBD that an ecosystem approach has specific characteristics. For example, the CoP adopted Decision V/6 entitled 'Ecosystem approach', in which Principle 5 emphasised the '[c]onservation of ecosystem structure and functioning' and that this 'should be a priority of the ecosystem approach'.[98] Similarly, Principle 6 stipulated that '[e]cosystems must be managed within the limits of their functioning'[99] and Principle 7 that '[t]he ecosystem approach should be undertaken at the appropriate spatial and temporal scales'.[100]

Part IV of the UN Watercourses Convention 1997 suggests in several aspects that an ecosystem approach is to be adopted.[101] Article 20 takes a holistic approach in the way that it deals with ecosystems, fish and aquatic species, as well as other living resources. This means that the entire watercourse area is understood as intrinsically connected and regulated as such. Moreover, the ILC has commented that

> the general obligation of equitable participation demands that the contributions of watercourse States to joint protection and preservation efforts be at least proportional to the measure in which they have contributed to the threat or harm to ecosystems in question.[102]

The ILC has also defined an ecosystem as an 'ecological unit consisting of living and non-living components that are interdependent and function as a community'[103] and, in the context of the drafting of the UN Watercourses Convention, the term 'ecosystem' was opted for over the term environment because it was considered to be more precise. The ILC noted that the term 'environment'

> could be interpreted quite broadly, to apply to areas 'surrounding' the watercourse that have only a minimal bearing on the protection and preservation of the watercourse itself. Furthermore, the term 'environment' of a watercourse might be construed to refer only to areas outside the watercourse, which is of course not the intention of the Commission. For these reasons, the Commission preferred to utilise the term 'ecosystem' which is believed to have a more precise scientific and legal meaning.[104]

The *travaux préparatoires* of the UN Watercourses Convention reveal that there was some debate over the inclusion of the term 'ecosystem'. Those advocating a restrictive approach to the environmental protection that the Convention offers put forward the phrase 'ecological balance'. Ultimately, however, the term ecosystem was decided upon and put in the Preamble and Article 20.[105]

The Expert Consultant to the General Assembly Working Group on the UN Watercourses Convention, Robert Rosenstock, explained that '[t]he concept of biodiversity was included in the notion of ecosystems as defined in the commentary and in the Biodiversity Convention'.[106] Similarly, he was of the opinion that the regeneration of ecosystems 'was addressed in Article 21 in that prevention, reduction and control of pollution referred to the restoration of the *status quo ante*'.[107] The ILC commentary to Article 21 sets out that the obligation to protect 'requires that watercourse States shield ecosystems of international watercourses from harm or damage' and 'includes the duty to protect those ecosystems from a significant threat of harm'.[108] This all lends support to the proposition that an ecosystem approach is to be adopted in general when interpreting the provisions of the UN Watercourses Convention.

These examples all represent a strong endorsement of the ecosystem approach in multilateral environmental agreements and other instruments of international environmental law. The approach takes account of the wide variety of possible damage and the evolving nature of scientific understanding around the interconnected nature of the environment.

Concluding remarks

This chapter has considered various regimes for environmental compensation that exist at the international level. The UNCC F4 panel administered environmental claims within an institutional structure and did much to develop understandings of environmental harm and valuation techniques.

The IOPC Funds regime similarly features an institutional structure that oversees the assessment of environmental harm, provides for liability and has also developed a funding system where the actor found liable for environmental harm cannot cover the costs of restoration. This and other liability regimes have traditionally been restrictive in their approach to environmental harm, but such an approach appears to have changed with more recent regimes. Indeed, understandings of environmental harm or pollution have evolved from liability for damage to property and persons and economic loss to liability for damage to the environment as such. The oil pollution regime has fallen into the first category, while deep sea mining and Antarctica fall into the second. Moreover, newer treaties on climate change, biodiversity, watercourses and other aspects of the environment embrace a broader notion of environmental harm, in particular with an emphasis on damage to ecosystems.

Notes

1 Security Council Resolution 687 (1991), UN Doc. S/RES/687 (1991), para 16.
2 Tarcisio Hardman Reis, *Compensation for Environmental Damages under International Law* (Wolters Kluwer, 2011), 60.
3 UNCC, https://uncc.ch/home.
4 UNCC, 'Follow-Up Programme for Environmental Awards', https://uncc.ch/follow-programme-environmental-awards-0.
5 See, for example, Daniel Farber, 'The UNCC as a Model for Climate Compensation' in Cymie R. Payne and Peter H. Sand (eds.), *Gulf War Reparations and the UN Compensation Commission* (Oxford University Press, 2011), 242; Laurence Boisson de Chazournes and Danio Campanelli, 'The United Nations Compensation Commission: Time for an Assessment?' in Andreas Fischer-Lescano et al. (eds.), *Frieden in Freiheit = Peace in liberty = Paix en liberté: Festschrift für Michael Bothe zum 70 Geburtstag* (Nomos, 2008), 14.
6 Cymie R. Payne, 'Developments in the Law of Environmental Reparations: A Case Study of the UN Compensation Commission' in Carsten Stahn, Jens Iverson, and Jennifer Easterday (eds.), *Environmental Protection and Transitions from Conflict to Peace: Clarifying Norms, Principles and Practices* (Oxford University Press, 2017), 341–2.
7 UNCC Governing Council Decision 7, Criteria for Additional Categories of Claims, UN Doc. S/AC.26/1991/7/Rev.1, para 37.
8 UNCC, *Report and Recommendations Made By the Panel of Commissioners Concerning Part One of the Fourth Instalment of 'F4' Claims* (9 December 2004), UN Doc. S/AC.26/2004/16, para 354.
9 Payne, 'Developments in the Law of Environmental Reparations: A Case Study of the UN Compensation Commission', op cit, 346.
10 Mojtaba Kazazi, 'An Overview of Evidence before the United Nations Compensation Commission' 1 (1999) *International Law Forum* 219, 223.
11 See Michael Huguenin, Michael Donlan, Alexandra van Geel and Robert Paterson, 'Assessment and Valuation of Damage to the Environment' in Payne

and Sand (eds.), *Gulf War Reparations and the UN Compensation Commission*, op cit, 83.

12 UNCC, *Report and Recommendations Made By the Panel of Commissioners Concerning the Fifth Instalment of 'F4' Claims* (30 June 2005), UN Doc. S/AC.26/2005/10, paras 329 and 266; UNCC, *Report and Recommendations Made By the Panel of Commissioners Concerning the Fourth Instalment of 'F4' Claims* (9 December 2004), op cit, para 78.

13 UNCC, *Report and Recommendations Made By the Panel of Commissioners Concerning the Fifth Instalment of 'F4' Claims*, op cit, paras 170–8.

14 UNCC, 'Follow-Up Programme for Environmental Awards', https://uncc.ch/follow-programme-environmental-awards-0.

15 UNCC, *Report and Recommendations Made By the Panel of Commissioners Concerning the Fifth Instalment of 'F4' Claims*, op cit, paras 61, 86–99, 106–11, 121–5, 134–8.

16 Ibid., paras 62, 64–74.

17 UNCC, *Report and Recommendations Made By the Panel of Commissioners Concerning Part One of the Fourth Instalment of 'F4' Claims*, op cit, paras 68, 70–1, 105–8.

18 Payne, 'Developments in the Law of Environmental Reparations: A Case Study of the UN Compensation Commission', op cit, 332.

19 UNCC, *Governing Council, Report and Recommendations Made By the Panel of Commissioners Concerning the Fifth Instalment of 'F4' Claims*, op cit, para 57.

20 Ibid., para 5.

21 Payne, 'Developments in the Law of Environmental Reparations: A Case Study of the UN Compensation Commission', op cit, 354.

22 UNCC, *Governing Council, Report and Recommendations Made By the Panel of Commissioners Concerning the Fifth Instalment of 'F4' Claims*, op cit, para 81.

23 Ibid., para 80.

24 UNCC, *Report and Recommendations Made By the Panel of Commissioners Concerning Part One of the Fourth Instalment of 'F4' Claims*, op cit, para 446.

25 Ibid., paras 325–8, 362.

26 Ibid., paras 174–81.

27 See UNCC, Governing Council Decision 7, op cit, para 35.

28 Ibid., para 54.

29 See Payne, 'Developments in the Law of Environmental Reparations: A Case Study of the UN Compensation Commission', op cit, 347.

30 UNCC, *Report and Recommendations Made By the Panel of Commissioners Concerning Part One of the Fourth Instalment of 'F4' Claims*, op cit, para 71.

31 Ibid., para 103–55.

32 UNCC, *Report and Recommendations Made By the Panel of Commissioners Concerning Part Two of the Fourth Instalment of 'F4' Claims*, op cit, para 25.

33 UNCC, *Report and Recommendations Made By the Panel of Commissioners Concerning the Third Instalment of 'F4' Claims* (18 December 2003), UN Doc. S/AC.26/2003/31, paras 169–89.

34 UNCC, *Report and Recommendations Made By the Panel of Commissioners Concerning the Fifth Instalment of 'F4' Claims*, op cit, paras 611–36.

35 See, for example: Jordan's claim regarding damaged rangeland and wildlife reserves that had been caused by traffic, overgrazing by the livestock of refugees and the plants that refuges had yielded for fuel; Kuwait's clam that ecological services in its desert had been damages by tarcrete, windblown sand, oil

pollution, fortifications and ordnance; UNCC, *Report and Recommendations Made By the Panel of Commissioners Concerning the Fifth Instalment of 'F4' Claims*, op cit, paras 362–3 and 413–75.

36 See, for example, Payne, 'Developments in the Law of Environmental Reparations: A Case Study of the UN Compensation Commission', op cit.

37 See, UNCC, *Report and Recommendations Made By the Panel of Commissioners Concerning the First Instalment of 'F4' Claims* (22 June 2001), UN Doc. S/AC.26/2001/16, para 42; Peter Sand, 'Environmental Dispute Settlement and the Experience of the UN Compensation Committee' 54 (2011) *Japanese Yearbook of International Law* 151, 170.

38 UNCC, Governing Council Decision 7, op cit.

39 Peter Sand, 'Environmental Principles Applied' in Payne and Sand (eds.), *Gulf War Reparations and the UN Compensation Commission*, op cit, 170–2.

40 Huguenin, Donlan, van Geel and Paterson, 'Assessment and Valuation of Damage to the Environment', op cit, 92.

41 See Peter Sand, 'Compensation for Environmental Damage from the 1991 Gulf War' 35 (2005) *Environmental Policy and Law* 244.

42 See Farber, 'The UNCC as a Model for Climate Compensation', op cit, 249–50.

43 Article 1(6) CLC.

44 IOPC Fund, Resolution No. 3 – Pollution Damage (October 1980).

45 See IOPC Funds, 'Incidents', www.iopcfunds.org/incidents/incident-map/.

46 Preamble, International Convention on the Establishment of an International Fund for Compensation for Oil Pollution Damage 1992.

47 See IOPC Funds, 'Compensation and Claims Management', https://iopcfunds.org/compensation/.

48 Ibid.

49 Huguenin, Donlan, van Geel and Paterson, 'Assessment and Valuation of Damage to the Environment', op cit, 70.

50 Ibid.

51 Louise de La Fayette, 'The Concept of Environmental Damage in International Liability Regimes' in Michael Bowman and Alan Boyle (eds.), *Environmental Damage in International and Comparative Law: Problems of Definition and Valuation* (Oxford University Press, 2002), 158–9; IOPC Fund Doc. 92FUND/WGR.3/11 (5 March 2002).

52 IOPC, Resolution No. 3 – Pollution Damage (October 1980).

53 Article 1(a)(i), Convention on Third Party Liability in the Field of Nuclear Energy of 29 July 1960, as amended by the Additional Protocol of 28 January 1964 and by the Protocol of 16th November 1982.

54 See International Atomic Energy Agency, *The 1997 Vienna Convention on Civil Liability for Nuclear Damage and the 1997 Convention on Supplementary Compensation for Nuclear Damage – Explanatory Texts*, IAEA International Law Series No. 3 (IAEA, 2007), 1.

55 Ibid., 2.

56 Article 10, Protocol to Amend the Vienna Convention Civil Liability for Nuclear Damage 36 ILM 1454 (12 September 1997).

57 See International Atomic Energy Agency, *The 1997 Vienna Convention on Civil Liability for Nuclear Damage and the 1997 Convention on Supplementary Compensation for Nuclear Damage – Explanatory Texts*, IAEA International Law Series No. 3 (IAEA, 2007), 2.

58 Canada: Claim against the Union of Soviet Republics for Damage Caused by Soviet Cosmos 954 18(4) (1979) ILM 899.

59 Ibid., 899 and 905.
60 Protocol between Government of Canada and the Government of the Union of Soviet Socialist Republics, 2 April 1981 (1981) 20 ILM 689.
61 UN GA Resolution 47/68 on 'Principles Relevant to the Use of Nuclear Power Sources in Outer Space'.
62 Ibid., para 3.
63 International Law Association, Space Law Committee, *Report of the London Conference* (July 2000), 4.
64 See Silja Vöneky, 'The Liability Annex to the Protocol on Environmental Protection to the Antarctic Treaty' in Doris König, Peter-Tobias Stoll, Volker Röben, and Nele Matz-Lück (eds.), *International Law Today: New Challenges and the Need for Reform?* (Springer, 2007), 166.
65 Article 1(1), UNCLOS 1982.
66 See, for example, Articles 145 and 194 UNCLOS 1982.
67 Adopted by the ISA Assembly on 13 July 2000.
68 de La Fayette, 'Environmental Damage in International Liability Regimes', op cit, 177.
69 International Seabed Authority, Standard Clauses for Exploration Contract, https://ran-s3.s3.amazonaws.com/isa.org.jm/s3fs-public/documents/EN/Regs/Code-Annex4.pdf.
70 See UNFCCC Decision 2/CP.19: Warsaw International Mechanism for Loss and Damage Associated with Climate Change Impacts (2013); UNFCCC Adoption of the Paris Agreement FCCC/CP/2015/10/Add.1.1_32 (2015).
71 See paragraph 52 of the Decision of the Contracting Parties.
72 INC Vanuatu: Draft Annex Relating to Article 23 (Insurance) for inclusion in the revised single text on elements relating to mechanisms (A/AC.237/WG.II/Misc.13) (INC, 1991).
73 Decision 1/CP.21, Adoption of the Paris Agreement (FCCC/CP/2–15/10/Add.1), para 52.
74 Declarations of the Cook Islands, Marshall Islands, Nauru, Niue, Philippines, Solomon Islands, Tuvalu, and Vanuatu following the Paris Agreement (FCCC/CP/2–15/10/Add.1), https://treaties.un.org/pages/ViewDetails.aspx?src=IND&mtdsg_no=XXVII-7-d&chapter=27&lang=en.
75 Steve Vanderheiden, *Atmospheric Justice: A Political Theory of Climate Change* (Oxford University Press, 2009), 144; Maxine Burkett, 'A Justice Paradox: Climate Change, Small Island Developing States, and the Absence of International Legal Remedy' in Carmen Gonzales and Sumudu Atapattu (eds.), *International Environmental Law and the Global South* (Cambridge University Press, 2015).
76 See Petra Tschakert, Neville Ellis, Christopher Anderson, A. Kelly and James Obeng, 'One Thousand Ways to Experience Loss: A Systematic Analysis of Climate-Related Intangible Harm from around the World' 55 (2019) *Global Environmental Change* 58, 60.
77 Ibid., 62.
78 Ibid., 69.
79 Ibid.
80 See de La Fayette, 'Environmental Damage in International Liability Regimes', op cit, 167.
81 See, for example, Conclusions by the Working Group of Experts on Liability and Compensation for Environmental Damage Arising from Military Activities

in Aleksandr Timoshenko (ed.), *Liability and Compensation for Environmental Damage: Compilation of Documents* (UNEP, 1998).

82 Ibid.

83 Annex to decision SS.XI/5 B, Proceedings of the Governing Council/Global Ministerial Environment Forum at its eleventh special session, UNEP/GCSS. XI/11 (3 March 2010).

84 UNEP, Manual on Compliance With and Enforcement of Multilateral Environmental Agreements (2006), 350.

85 Edward Barbier, Michael Acreman and Duncan Knowler, *Economic Valuation of Wetlands: A Guide for Policy Makers and Planners* (Ramsar Convention Bureau, 1997).

86 See Charles De Visscher, 'La Contribution de l'Institut de Droit International au développement du droit international' in *Institut de Droit International, Livre du Centenaire 1873–1973: Evolution et Perspectives du Droit International* 128 (Karger, 1973); Edvard Hambro, 'The Centenary of the Institut de Droit International' 43 (1973) *Nordisk Tidsskrift for International Ret* 9.

87 Institut de droit international, *Responsibility and Liability under International Law for Environmental Damage* (Strasbourg, 1997).

88 *Certain Activities Carried Out By Nicaragua in the Border Area (Costa Rica v. Nicaragua) (Compensation)*, ICJ General List No. 150 (2 February 2018), Dissenting Opinion of Judge Ad Hoc Dugard, 8.

89 *Annuaire de l'Institut de droit international*, Final Report (Pedone, 1996) 339.

90 UNEP, *Report of the Working Group of Experts on Liability and Compensation for Environmental Damage Arising from Military Activities* (1996); ILC, *11th Report on International Liability for Injurious Consequences*, UN Doc. A/CN.4/468 (1995); ECE Convention on the Transboundary Effects of Industrial Accidents 1992; ECE Convention on Civil Liability for Damage Resulting from Accidents Dangerous to the Environment 1993.

91 ILC, Draft Articles on Responsibility of States for Internationally Wrongful Acts with commentaries 2001, II(2) YBILC (2001) and Commentaries, 101.

92 UNEP, *Liability and Compensation for Environmental Damage: Report of the Meeting of 8 August 2002*, UN Doc. UNEP/DEPI/L7C Expert Meeting 1/1.

93 UNEP, *Draft Guidelines for the Development of National Legislation on Liability, Response Action and Compensation for Damage Caused By Activities Dangerous to the Environment* (16–20 February 2009), UN Doc. UNEP/ GC.25/11/Add.2.

94 On the 'ecosystems approach', see for example George Francis, 'Ecosystem Management' (1993) 33 *Natural Resources Journal* 315; Ludwik Teclaff and Eileen Teclaff, 'International Control of Cross-Media Pollution: An Ecosystem Approach' 27 (1987) *Natural Resources Journal* 21.

95 Jutta Brunnée and Stephen Toope, 'Environmental Security and Freshwater Resources: A Case for International Ecosystem Law' 5 (1994) *Yearbook of International Environmental Law* 41, 55

96 See Jason Rudall, 'The Interplay between the UN Watercourses Convention and International Environmental Law' in Laurence Boisson de Chazournes, Makane Mbengue, Mara Tignino, Komlan Sangbana, and Jason Rudall (eds), *The UN Convention on the Law of Non-Navigational Uses of International Watercourses* (Oxford University Press, 2018); Owen McIntyre, 'Protection and Preservation of Freshwater Ecosystems (Articles 20-23)', op cit.

97   Including the decisions adopted by the Conferences of the Contracting Parties, e.g. 'Conservation, Integrated Management, and Sustainable Use of Mangrove Ecosystems and Their Resources', Resolution VIII.32, 8th Meeting of the Conference of the Contracting Parties to the Convention on Wetlands (Ramsar, 1971), Valencia, Spain, 18–26 November 2002.

98   Decisions Adopted by the Conference of the Parties to the Convention on Biological Diversity at its Fifth Meeting, Nairobi (15–26 May 2000), UN Doc. UNEP/CBD/COP/5/23, at 106.

99   Ibid.

100   Ibid.

101   For a complete consideration, see Rudall, 'The Interplay between the UN Watercourses Convention and International Environmental Law' in Boisson de Chazournes, Mbengue, Tignino, Sangbana, and Rudall (eds.), *The UN Convention on the Law of the Non-Navigational Uses of International Watercourses: A Commentary*, op cit; McIntyre, 'Protection and Preservation of Freshwater Ecosystems (Articles 20–23)', op cit; Laurence Boisson de Chazournes, *Fresh Water in International Law* (Oxford University Press, 2013).

102   ILC, Report of the International Law Commission on the Work of its Forty-Sixth Session, II(2) *YBILC* (1994), 282–3.

103   Ibid., 118.

104   Ibid., 280.

105   See, for example, UN Doc. A/C.6/51/SR.60 (1997).

106   UN General Assembly, Summary Record of the 21st Meeting, UN Doc. A/C.6/51/SR.21 (1996), 12.

107   Ibid.

108   ILC, Report of the International Law Commission on the Work of its Forty-Sixth Session, op cit, 119.

4 Environmental compensation in domestic and regional practice

Introduction

Developed regimes for environmental compensation exist in domestic and regional legal systems. There is also a wealth of case law under these regimes that provides an insight into the legal principles governing the award of environmental compensation. In this chapter, a focus is placed on the European Union (EU) and United States (US) to give a snapshot of the approach taken in domestic and regional approaches. There are, however, many other legal systems that address compensation for environmental harm.[1] The chapter also considers the recent groundswell in climate litigation and foresees the need for clarifying environmental compensation in this context.

Environmental liability and compensation in the European Union

Directive 2004/35/EC of the European Parliament and Council of 21 April 2004 provides for a framework on environmental liability for damage to the environment. It is known as the Directive on Environmental Liability with Regard to the Prevention and Remedying of Environmental Damage (Environmental Liability Directive or ELD) and provides for 'any remedial measure taken in relation to natural resources and/or services to compensate for the fact that primary remediation does not result in fully restoring the damaged natural resources and/or services'.[2]

Liability is incurred under the regime with respect to certain occupational activities that present a risk to the environment or human health, as well as activities where an operator is at fault or has been negligent. The regime is based on the polluter-pays principle, which is also provided for in Article 191(2) of the Treaty on the Functioning of the European Union. EU Member States should follow this Directive in their national legal systems.

Environmental damage is defined under the ELD as damage to certain protected species and natural habitats, damage to water and damage to soil. A strict liability regime is created for those who conduct dangerous activities, which are listed in Annex III of the ELD. Where other activities that are not listed under Annex III are carried out, an actor may be liable for damage to the environment, provided fault is proven. Article 8(1) provides that '[t]he operator shall bear the costs for the preventive and remedial actions taken pursuant to this Directive'. Article 8(2) goes on to set out that operators shall be required to pay 'costs . . . incurred in relation to the preventive or remedial actions taken under this Directive'. Remedial actions and costs relating thereto should be taken to restore the environment to its baseline condition. The ELD provides that the baseline condition means 'the condition at the time of the damage of the natural resources and services that would have existed had the environmental damage not occurred, estimated on the basis of the best information available'.[3]

Compensation for environmental damage is also envisaged by the ELD. Compensation is permitted with respect to both primary remediation – which includes 'any remedial measure which returns the damaged natural resources and/or impaired services to, or towards, baseline condition' – and compensatory restoration. The latter is divided into two parts and includes compensatory remediation, which means 'any action taken to compensate for interim losses of natural resources and/or services that occur from the date of damage occurring until primary remediation has achieved its full effect', as well as complementary remediation, which means 'any remedial measure taken in relation to natural resources and/or services to compensate for the fact that primary remediation does not result in fully restoring the damaged natural resources and/or services'.[4] Moreover, the ELD provides for interim losses which

> result from the fact that the damaged natural resources and/or services are not able to perform their ecological functions or provide services to other natural resources or to the public until the primary or complementary measures have taken effect. It does not consist of financial compensation to members of the public.[5]

Under the ELD, resource to resource and service to service equivalence scaling approaches are preferred in the assessment or valuation of environmental damage. These include, for example, habitat equivalency analysis (HEA) and resource equivalency analysis (REA), which we will consider further in the next chapter.

The Resource Equivalency Methods for Assessing Environmental Damage in the EU (REMEDE) Toolkit has been developed in the ELD context as well.[6] This project, funded by the European Commission, aims to 'develop, test and disseminate methods for determining the scale of the remedial measures necessary to adequately offset environmental damage'.[7] The project and Toolkit have been developed by ecologists, economists and lawyers using the best practices in the EU and the US. It relies on compensation scaling using a so-called equivalency analysis. The Toolkit is a three-pronged approach:

1 Measure the debit (loss). Assess the environmental injury and the subsequent economic damages over time.
2 Identify credits (gains). Identify feasible compensation projects designed to improve the injured resource over time.
3 Scale compensation. Determine 'how much is enough' compensation to ensure equivalence over time between debit and credit.[8]

Scaling requires the value of the debits to be equal to the value of the credits over time and will usually demand an assessment of value across time, space and other dimensions. It will take into account estimated values of non-market resources, such as biodiversity and certain ecosystem services. The REMEDE Toolkit sets out that an equivalency analysis involves five steps: (1) initial evaluation; (2) determining and quantifying the damage (the debit); (3) determining and quantifying the benefits of remediation (the credit); (4) scaling the complementary and compensatory remediation; and (5) monitoring and reporting.[9] Despite the preference for equivalency analysis, where it is not possible to perform HEA or REA, the ELD provides that other methods of scaling and valuation may be adopted.

Other EU directives, such as the Habitats Directive, the Birds Directive, the Environmental Impact Assessment (EIA) Directive and the Strategic Environmental Assessment (SEA) Directive also provide for environmental compensation, and the REMEDE Toolkit can be used in the context of these directives as well.[10] It is also likely that compensation for environmental damage will become ever more important for environmental regulation at the EU level. For example, the No Net Loss Initiative (NNL) sets out compensation as part of Action 7, Target 2 of the EU Biodiversity Strategy 2020.[11] This initiative is intended to ensure that there is no net loss of biodiversity and ecosystem services and aims to prevent a diminution in biodiversity and ecosystem services.[12] It should also be noted that, on 4 November 1998, the Council of Europe adopted a Convention on the Protection of the Environment through Criminal Law.[13] While encouraging the punishment of environmental crime, it does not prescribe the sanctions that must be taken and rather leaves this to be determined by state parties in their national legal systems.

Having sketched the fundamentals of the approach under EU law, we now turn to consider those pursued in the US.

Environmental liability and compensation in the United States

Under US law, the practice of valuing environmental damage is known as natural resource damage assessment.[14] The *Comprehensive Environmental Response, Compensation, and Liability Act 1980* forms part of the legislative framework governing environmental compensation or natural resource damages in the US. It allows trustees of environmental resources to seek compensation for damage to natural resources and is concerned with damage caused by hazardous substances, such as oil, as well as collateral injuries that may occur during the remediation of damage caused by hazardous substances.

The US Department of the Interior has issued regulations concerning the implementation of this legislation, and these list a number of acceptable techniques for appraising environmental damage, including conjoint analysis, habitat equivalency analysis, resource equivalency analysis and random utility modelling, although they do not exclude the possibility that others may similarly be appropriate.[15] More generally, the regulations set out four criteria for the acceptance of a method that evaluates environmental damage. These include feasibility and reliability, reasonable cost, avoidance of double counting and cost effectiveness.[16] Where alternatives exist for restoration, the regulations also provide for certain considerations, such as technical feasibility, a cost-benefit analysis, the risk of collateral environmental damage and the risk to human health and safety, as well as compliance with relevant legal and policy frameworks.

For environmental damage to have occurred under this regime, a measurable change in the environment or environmental services must be evident.[17] This might be shown, for example, in the context of damage to surface waters, by the collection of two water or sediment samples taken from different locations or at different times. While this will determine whether environmental damage has occurred, more substantial data is required for quantification of that damage.

Following the *Exxon Valdez* oil spill in 1989, the US decided not to become a party to the International Convention on Civil Liability for Oil Pollution Damage 1969 or the International Fund for Compensation for Oil Pollution Damage 1971 because neither were judged to provide sufficient compensation in cases like those involving the *Exxon Valdez* spill.[18] Indeed the cost of repairing the oil spill was much more than that available as compensation under the international regime. As a result, the US developed the Oil Pollution Act of 1990, which provided for higher amounts of compensation and allowed compensation for damage to the environment as such. Natural resource or environmental damage is defined under the Act as

> [d]amages for injury to, destruction of, loss of, or loss of use of, natural resources, including the reasonable costs of assessing the damage, which shall be recoverable by a United States trustee, a state trustee, an Indian tribe trustee, or a foreign trustee.[19]

Natural resources are defined under the Oil Pollution Act 1990 as including

> land, fish, wildlife, biota, air, water, drinking water supplies, and other such resources belonging to, managed by, held in trust by, appertaining to, or otherwise controlled by the United States (including the resources of exclusive economic zone), any state or local government or Indian tribe, or any foreign government.[20]

This legislative framework is concerned with damage that results from oil spills around US waters and on its shoreline, as well as in its Exclusive Economic Zone. It provides for the assessment of such damage, as well as compensation for restoration of the environmental damage and for interim losses incurred by the public. The latter can be estimated using resource to resource, service to service or valuation-based scaling approaches.[21] Moreover, in considering restoration, the alternatives should be evaluated as to cost, their potential to recover the environment to baseline condition, their capacity to compensate interim losses, their likely effectiveness, the risk of future damage to the environment, their potential to benefit several natural resources or environmental services and any potential public health and safety implications.[22]

Under the Oil Pollution Act of 1990, the National Oceanic and Atmospheric Administration has published several definitions that are helpful. Environmental damage or 'injury' is defined as 'an observable or measurable adverse change in a natural resource or impairment of a natural resource service. Injury may occur directly or indirectly to a natural resource and/or service'. Similarly, baseline environmental condition is defined under the Act as

> [t]he condition of the natural resources and services that would have existed had the incident not occurred. Baseline data may be estimated using historical data, reference data, control data, or data on incremental

changes (e.g., number of dead animals), alone or in combination, as appropriate.

Finally, restoration is defined as

> Any action . . . or combination of actions . . . to restore, rehabilitate, replace, or acquire the equivalent of injured natural resources and services. Restoration includes: (a) Primary restoration, which is any action, including natural recovery, that returns injured natural resources to baseline; and (b) Compensatory restoration, which is any action taken to compensate for interim losses of natural resources and services that occur from the date of the incident until recovery.[23]

The reasonable costs of assessing damages may also be compensated.

Under these regimes for environmental damage in the US, two forms of restoration activity are envisaged. These are primary restoration and compensatory restoration. The former are activities intended to restore the environment back to its baseline condition. The cost of this primary restoration is often a significant part of the compensation awarded. However, this may not take into account the loss of resource services that may result from the damage. The general public may suffer from this diminution in the quality or quantity of the resource. As a result, compensatory restoration is a regime designed to compensate for any interim or permanent losses incurred in this context. This value is normally calculated by reference to the cost of compensatory restoration projects, which should be constructed to replace the lost services that would otherwise be provided by the damaged resource.[24] Where ecological services that humans derive benefit from are lost (e.g., recreation fishing), initiatives should be taken that aim at improving the experience for those humans affected (e.g., alternative fishing sites, fish restocking, etc.). Where ecological services to the environment are lost, habitat equivalency analyses (HEA) are generally used.[25]

As will be explored further in the next chapter, HEA estimates the cost of replacement projects that provide equivalent ecosystem services. Economic discounting can be used to account for projected gains and losses in calculating the amount of restoration required. Compensation is then calculated by reference to the cost of implementing these replacement projects. HEA is thus used in both US and EU practice. That said, the practice has shown that it comes with challenges in terms of selecting input values and estimating environmental damage in the future.[26]

Interim services losses are also permissible under the US regime. This is generally adopted where the valuation of restoration costs is not possible.

Interim service losses can be calculated by recourse to market prices where such data is available – such as where the cost of using the resource has increased or the quantity of the resource that can be traded on the market has decreased – or by recourse to non-market valuation techniques where the resource is not traded on the market. The latter may include revealed preference methods –which are valuations based on consumer behaviour – or stated preference methods, which involves asking consumers to state the value they put on a given resource or activity.

Where none of the previous options are possible, some practice exists on the use of a benefits transfer approach. This approach takes existing valuations that have been conducted in different circumstances and adapts them to the present scenario.[27] This approach can vary in the accuracy of the estimates it provides depending on the circumstances in which it is being applied and the previous data collected. Guidance has been issued by US regulators on this approach.[28]

The US approach provides for compensation for the loss of use of natural resources as well as non-use value lost (such as appreciation for the existence of a natural resource) while the environment is being repaired. Moreover, under US legislation, during restoration, an equivalent site should be provided where the original site is significantly damaged. This is not the case in international regimes.

Environmental damage and compensation in the case law of domestic courts

Typically, courts and tribunals at the domestic level have three courses of action available to them as remedies for environmental harm. The first is penalties, fines or other punitive sanctions. The second is injunctive relief or an alternative to cease or redress the harm. The third is compensation for environmental harm.[29] As will be seen, domestic courts have had recourse to one or several of these remedies in any given case. For example, penalties may be ordered along with compensation for environmental harm. The penalties are punitive in nature while the compensation is restorative. Penalties are paid to the government for a violation of the law while compensation is paid directly or indirectly to those affected by the harm. A government may seek compensation in the public interest[30] and usually does so within a legislative framework. For example, the Environmental Damage Act of 2007 in Germany permits governmental agencies to sue an actor for pollution in order to obtain a remedy to repair environmental damage.[31]

Various approaches can be detected in selected case law from national jurisdictions concerning the evaluation of environmental damage and the awarding of compensation. Generally speaking, courts are becoming more amenable to recognising broader notions of damage and compensable values, such as ecological damage or damage to the environment per se.

In some cases, national courts have reasoned along the lines of economic loss through the application of a common rule of liability.[32] This was evident in the US case concerning the oil spill from the *Amoco Cadiz* oil tanker off the coast of France.[33] There, the Court stated that only economic damages would be recognised and, as a result, only these would be compensated.[34] This case of the US District Court for the Northern District of Illinois developed many categories of damage, from clean-up activities by public employees to the cost of using public buildings in the clean-up operation and from coastline and harbour restoration to the cost of ecological harm.[35]

The contingent valuation method was used in the proceedings of the case concerning the *Exxon Valdez* oil spill in 1989.[36] The contingent valuation method is based on assessing willingness to pay by asking a statistically chosen set of persons, using questionnaire techniques, what they would be willing to pay for a benefit. It will be elaborated upon in the next chapter. This method was used when the State of Alaska requested a valuation be conducted following the spill from the oil tanker. While the case was settled out of court for USD1.15 billion, it has been argued that the study was one reason for settling the claim since it valued the environmental damage at USD3 billion on the basis of the contingent valuation method.[37]

In a case involving an oil spill from the USSR vessel *Antonio Gramsci*, a court in the USSR used a mathematical method known as *methodika*, which is based on a fixed amount of compensation being paid for every cubic metre of seawater polluted.[38] This approach was provided for under Soviet law. However, the case involved a payment under the IOPC Fund regime, and the IOPC rejected such a method of calculation. Subsequently, the IOPC adopted a resolution objecting to the use of 'abstract quantification based on theoretical models'.[39] Parties to the CLC and Fund Conventions insisted that pollution damage under the conventions meant that compensation was limited to the costs of reasonable measures taken for repair of the environment.

In the *Patmos* case of 1985, which concerned an oil spill from a tanker, a claim was brought by the Italian government against the IOPC Fund based on the CLC 1969.[40] The Italian government sought compensation for damage to marine flora and fauna or, in other words, for pure environmental damage. The Italian government claimed it was a trustee for the national patrimony, which encompasses the environment. This claim was initially rejected by the Fund and also by the Court of First Instance of Messina before being accepted by the relevant Court of Appeal, which awarded the government compensation for ecological damages. The amount did not exceed the amount of the shipowner's liability, and so the IOPC Fund did not have to pay out.

Similarly, the *Haven Case* concerned an oil spill after a tanker caught fire and sank in 1991. This involved a claim in an Italian court, which held that compensation under the CLC 1969 and the IOPC Fund 1971 could be for pure environmental damage and that the Italian government could be the trustee of the national patrimony, which encompasses the environment. That said, the Italian national court could not quantify the environmental damage economically, and so an amount was ordered by the judge on the basis of equitable considerations. Because this amount exceeded the shipowner's liability, the IOPC did have to pay out in this case. As a result, the IOPC sought a settlement.[41]

In other cases, compensation has been calculated on the basis of the cost of replacing natural resources. For example, in the case of *Commonwealth of Puerto Rico v. The MV Zoe Colocotroni*, where the captain had ordered the dumping of 5,000 tonnes of crude oil into the waters after his ship ran aground, a US court awarded damages based on the costs involved in replacing the millions of aquatic organisms destroyed by the spill. In doing so it rejected a proposed measure based on the loss of market value of the affected area. Rather, it reasoned that the appropriate methodology would be based on the reasonable costs incurred by the State to restore the environment to the pre-existing condition.[42] However, the court had also rejected as grossly disproportionate an assessment of compensation that included the replacement of damaged trees and sediments, in addition to other restoration costs.[43] This grossly disproportionate costs threshold was latterly reflected in the US legislative framework on natural resource damages, (i.e., the OPA 1990 and CERCLA 1988 as discussed earlier). This case was also important as it provided guidance as to assessing the appropriate restoration of the damaged environment. The court said the relevant factors for consideration were technical feasibility, harmful side effects, interaction with natural regeneration, effectiveness of measures and proportionality of costs.[44]

The case of *State of Ohio v. US Department of the Interior* concerned a judicial review of the regulations on natural resource damages issued by the US Department of the Interior (DOI) under the CERCLA 1988.[45] In this case, the regulations issued by the DOI were invalidated in part by the court because some of the regulations limited recovery to lost use values by market pricing, rather than the value of restoring or replacing natural resources, which was the object of CERCLA. The court stated that the 'DOI should consider a rule that would permit the trustees to derive use value for natural resources by summing up all reliably calculated use values, however measured, so long as the trustee does not double count'. Such use values should not only include consumptive use values. The court indicated that the DOI should also consider the inclusion of non-consumptive values, such as existence (the value derived from knowing an environmental recourse exists) or option values (the value of potential future uses of environmental resources). The court did uphold the DOI's reliance on the contingent valuation method in its regulations and noted that the DOI was permitted to rank valuation techniques based on their perceived reliability.[46]

A benefits transfer approach was used in the litigation concerning the *American Trader*, which spilled oil in the Pacific Ocean causing damage to a number of beaches in California. The litigation took place in 1997 and involved the State of California and Attransco, a company that operated vessels for the marine transportation of freight. The State of California had to calculate the number of beach days lost as well as the value of a lost beach day. The State of California relied on a benefits transfer approach to calculate the value of each lost trip. A study on the value of beach days in Florida was used and adjusted for inflation. The State of California estimated on this basis that the cost of a beach day was USD13.19 per trip. As such, they calculated that the value of lost beach days in total was USD10,188,500. Moreover, the lost fishing and whale watching possibilities were factored into the calculation, which they valued at USD1.2 million using a benefits transfer approach once again.[47] Later the total estimate was revised to USD14.5 million. Attransco, on the other hand, disputed the statistical model used by the claimants to calculate the lost beach days, which they claimed had been overestimated. Moreover, they used a contingent valuation method to study the value of a beach day at beaches on the Californian coast, arriving at an amount of USD2.17 to USD3.38 per trip. They did not factor in travel costs, however, which may have led to estimates between USD8 and USD60 per trip.[48] Nevertheless, Attransco estimated the total amount of loss at USD607,200.

The Court ultimately awarded damages to the State of California in the amount of USD12.7 million for the lost recreation value, and USD5.3 million in civil liability as well as USD4.37 million in costs.[49] This is a good example of a domestic court recognizing the value of non-market values, like recreation as in this case.

The *Erika* case in France was the first time that purely ecological damage had been recognised in French civil liability law.[50] This case involved the sinking of the *Erika* oil tanker, a Maltese-registered vessel, off the coast of Brittany in France in 1999 and resulting in a massive oil spill causing vast environmental damage.

This vessel had been constructed in 1975 and was therefore nearly 25 years old at the time of the incident. However, the *Erika* was a cost-effective ship to run as it was much lighter than more modern tankers, which were made of more robust steel. For this reason, oil companies liked to avail of the *Erika* for transporting their cargos. Several ships of its kind had already been flagged as problematic for the structural deficiencies that they had prior to the spill. The *Erika* broke in half during a strong storm and spilt 19,800 tonnes of oil. Around 400km of coastline was affected, more than 50,000 birds were killed and the restoration work took three months.

The French Supreme Court handed down its decision on 25 September 2012 and found all four defendants – TOTAL SA as the charterer, the classification society RINA, the manager of Tevere Shipping as owner and the manager of Panship as technical manager – criminally liable for the pollution caused by the oil spill. Interestingly, the Supreme Court thus went beyond Article III of the CLC 1992 regime, which channels liability to the owner of the vessel exclusively.

The defendants in the case were held jointly and severally liable for around Eur200 million in damages.[51] The polluters were obliged to pay compensation to regional councils and municipalities who had been involved in the clean-up process for ecological damage. This included regions, departments and communities that had been affected by the oil spill.[52] It also awarded the League for the Protection of Birds (an NGO) Eur300,000 for ecological prejudice.

It should also be pointed out that punitive damages were imposed in this case. The oil company TOTAL had to pay Eur375,000 as a fine for maritime pollution, which was the maximum under French law. Moreover, the owner of the *Erika* and the president of its managing company each had to pay Eur75,000, which was similarly the maximum penalty that could be imposed on individuals. The Italian authority that certified the *Erika* as seaworthy was fined Eur175,000.[53]

The French Civil Code was latterly amended to include the concept of ecological damage.[54] Article 1246 of the Biodiversity Law 2016 provides that '[a]ll persons responsible for "ecological damage" must repair the injury' while Article 1247 limits ecological damage to 'a significant breach of elements or functions of ecosystems or collective benefits derived by humans from the environment'. Article 1248 sets out that

> [a]n action for 'ecological damage' is open to anyone with the capacity and interest to take actions including the State, the French Agency for biodiversity, local communities, and groups whose territory is concerned and public institutions and associations, licensed or created for at least five years from the date of the commencement of the proceedings that aim to protect nature and the environment.[55]

While reparation of the environment is preferred, where this is not possible, damages must still be paid under the Biodiversity Law.

The Swedish Supreme Court has also recognised compensation for loss of ecological value.[56] In a case involving the unlawful killing of two wolverines, the Swedish government claimed compensation for the loss of the endangered animals. In valuing the ecological damage, the lower courts of Sweden had looked to their recreational value and concluded that compensation should be based on this amount as this was the economic loss suffered.[57] While confirming the awards of the lower courts, which had awarded SEK20,000 for each wolverine, the Supreme Court took a different approach. It recognised that the wolverines were an endangered species and that the government was under an obligation to protect and conserve the wolverines. The Court also observed that the harm caused had both economic and non-economic aspects. While the wolverines did not have economic value per se, there were costs involved in their conservation that were wasted because of their killing. Reasonable compensation should be based on the breeding value of the wolverines, with the conservation expenses taken as a minimum value.[58] Since then environmental compensation has been defined in Sweden as

> the requirement that those who cause environmental injury to the natural environment – including public resources such as species, natural habitats, ecosystem functions, and user values – should offset these losses by creating new values with the explicit aim of avoiding a net loss.[59]

The oil spill by the oil rig *Deepwater Horizon* in the Gulf of Mexico on 20 April 2010[60] involved the escape of about 3.19 million barrels of oil in the Gulf of Mexico and an explosion killed 11 workers on the fixed oil rig located 50 miles from the cost of the US. It took almost three months to stem the flow of oil into the sea. The coasts of Florida, Alabama, Mississippi, Louisiana and Texas were all affected. It is considered to be the largest oil spill that the oil industry has ever experienced and the worst environmental disaster in US history. British Petroleum (BP) was the operator of the rig.

In 2018, BP estimated that it had paid out almost USD65 billion in legal fees, settlements and funding clean-up and restoration activities.[61] To settle claims, a Court Supervised Settlement Program was established after the disaster to deal with the approximately 400,000 cases that resulted. It reached a settlement for federal and state claims of USD19 billion in July 2015. State and federal agencies used intensive scientific methods to assess the impacts of the spill and to formulate a comprehensive restoration plan. An ecosystems services approach has been adopted in the restoration approach. In accordance with the plan, the concerned agencies have allocated USD4.7 billion to the restoration and conservation of habitats, USD410 million to restoring the water quality, USD1.8 billion to replenishing and protecting coastal living resources, USD420 million to providing and enhancing recreational opportunities and USD1.5 billion to monitoring, adaptive management and oversight.[62]

These cases and incidents provide an insight into the way in which domestic courts and authorities have approached the assessment and valuation of environmental damage. On the basis of this study, in some jurisdictions it is possible to see an evolution towards a recognition of compensation for environmental damage per se, as well as the value of species and ecosystems. We now turn to consider other developments concerning environmental protection in the courts and tribunals of domestic jurisdictions.

Environmental courts and tribunals

In some countries, specialised environmental courts exist. This is a relatively recent development. These can vary from administrative tribunals like the Environmental Appeals Board of the US Environmental Protection Agency, superior courts of record like Australia's New South Wales Land and Environment Court, the Environmental Court of New Zealand, Chinese provincial environmental courts or India's National Green Tribunal.[63] The latter has jurisdiction over the entire country, and its decisions can be appealed to the Indian Supreme Court. These fora have specialised judges, lawyers and technical experts that allow them to render high-quality decisions on complex environmental matters.[64] These courts also serve to make the litigation of environmental courts more efficient, centralise jurisdiction and often offer multiple forms of (alternative) dispute resolution.[65] These courts can also have wide ranging jurisdiction. For example, Guatemala established an environmental court in 2015, which has jurisdiction over claims concerning ecocide. It has already rendered a decision ordering a suspension of operations by a palm oil plantation owner who had killed large quantities of fish after dumping palm oil effluent in a river, in turn affecting 12,000 people along the river.[66] The expertise and efficiency that such tribunals offer is likely to benefit environmental protection and could be a model for other jurisdictions.

A further development that is interesting to note in the domestic context is the rise in climate litigation.

Climate change litigation

There has been a steady increase in litigation on the climate in domestic and regional jurisdictions.[67] These cases have been brought on various bases. For example, in the United States the Clean Air Act,[68] the public nuisance doctrine[69] and the public trust doctrine[70] have all been bases for litigation. In

Canada, the UNFCCC and the Kyoto Protocol have been the subject of certain cases.[71] In Pakistan, principles of sustainable development, precaution and inter-generational equity have been invoked in climate litigation.[72] In Nigeria, human rights law has been the foundation of certain cases[73] while in New Zealand domestic environmental legislation has been the source of claims related to climate change.[74] However, this domestic litigation over the last 15 years has borne mixed results.

More recently, several domestic and regional developments are especially notable. In the Netherlands, a Dutch national court has ordered the government to reduce emissions so that its citizens may be protected from climate change.[75] In particular, it stipulated the Dutch government must be more ambitious in its emission reduction targets. This case, *Urgenda*, was brought under human rights and tort law as a climate liability suit. The judge warned that the threat posed by global warming was acute and that the Dutch government had committed to act through international treaties. The judge noted specifically that the State should not hide behind the argument that the solution to the global climate problem does not depend solely on Dutch efforts.[76]

At the regional level, too, there are interesting developments. The Court of Justice of the European Union has previously dealt with climate change-related issues,[77] but presently before the Court is the so-called 'People's Climate Case',[78] which represents the first ever EU-wide climate court case. In this case, 10 families from Portugal, Germany, France, Italy, Romania, Kenya, Fiji and the Saami Youth Association brought a suit against the European Parliament and European Council. They claim that the EU's emissions target to reduce domestic greenhouse gas emissions was inadequate. They argue that the EU's climate policies do not protect their fundamental rights and are materially damaging their lives and livelihoods. Their claim is anchored in the principles of equality and sustainable development, the no-harm principle and the EU's environmental policy. Their case was initially dismissed by the European General Court, but on 11 July 2019, the plaintiffs filed an appeal.[79] While dismissing their initial case, the European General Court nevertheless accepts that the families and Saami Youth who filed the case were affected by climate change.[80] That said, the first instance court was of the view that they did not meet the direct and individual concern criterion under EU law given that climate change is likely to affect a wide range of people.[81]

With all Member States of the EU implicated in this case, there has not been a case on this scale involving the climate to date. Whether the case will succeed is difficult to predict, however, especially given the various hurdles that have to be surmounted.

While this litigation generally concerns government climate targets, in particular a lack of ambition in setting targets or failure to meet set targets, it is nevertheless part of the broader picture on the environment in courts and tribunals. Combined with the expanding notions of jurisdiction and connection between human rights and environmental degradation sketched out in Chapter 2, domestic courts may very well become popular fora for the litigation of climate damages and compensation.

Concluding remarks

The ELD and US legislative framework concerning environmental damage assessment and valuation adopt a variety of techniques for calculating environmental compensation. An emphasis is placed on HEA and REA approaches, as well as compensating losses in the short term while longer term restoration takes place. Domestic case law and other practice shows a move towards compensation for environmental harm per se. Moreover, as is evident from some municipal legal systems and cases, notional or non-market-based valuation techniques have been used. It is also important to highlight that, in certain legal systems, specialised environmental courts and tribunals are being set up to deal with cases involving environmental harm. These possess specific expertise on environmental matters. Finally, the phenomenon of climate litigation brings into sharp focus the need for refining the practice of environmental compensation, as well as concepts of environmental damage that encompass the impact such harm can have in terms of climate degradation and the impairment of human rights.

Notes

1 For insights into these systems, see Tseming Yang, Anastasia Telesetsky, Lin Harmon-Walker and Robert V. Percival, *Comparative and Global Environmental Law and Policy* (Wolters Kluwer, 2019); Michael Bowman and Alan Boyle (eds.), *Environmental Damage in International and Comparative Law: Problems of Definition and Valuation* (Oxford University Press, 2001), chaps 10–19.
2 European Parliament and Council Directive 2004/35/CE of 21 April 2004 on Environmental Liability with Regard to the Prevention and Remedying of Environmental Damage.
3 Article 2(14), ibid.
4 Annex II, 1(a)-(c), ibid.
5 Annex II, 1(d), ibid.
6 REMEDE, 'Welcome', www.envliability.eu.
7 REMEDE, 'About REMEDE', www.envliability.eu/about.htm.
8 Norden, *Environmental Compensation: Key Conditions for Increased and Cost Effective Application* (Nordic Council of Ministers, 2015), www.greengrowth knowledge.org/sites/default/files/downloads/resource/Environmental_compen sation_Norden.pdf.
9 REMEDE, 'Main Toolkit', www.envliability.eu/docs/D13MainToolkit_and_ Annexes/REMEDE_D13_Toolkit_310708.pdf.
10 REMEDE, 'Welcome', www.envliability.eu.

11 Action 7 under target 2 of the EU Biodiversity Strategy 2020.
12 Ibid.
13 Convention on the Protection of the Environment through Criminal Law 1998 (ETS No. 172).
14 Michael Huguenin, Michael Donlan, Alexandra van Geel and Robert Paterson, 'Assessment and Valuation of Damage to the Environment' in Cymie R. Payne and Peter H. Sand (eds.), *Gulf War Reparations and the UN Compensation Commission* (Oxford University Press, 2011), at 69.
15 43 CFR Part 11.
16 Ibid.
17 Ibid.
18 See Rep No. 94, 101st Congress 1st Session 2 (1989).
19 S. 2701(2), Oil Pollution Act 1990.
20 S. 1001(2), ibid.
21 15 CFR Part 990.
22 Ibid.
23 Ibid.
24 See Huguenin, Donlan, van Geel and Paterson, 'Assessment and Valuation of Damage to the Environment', op cit, 77–8.
25 Ibid., 78. See also, Robert Unworth and Richard Bishop, 'Assessing Natural Resource Damages Using Environmental Annuities' 11 (1994) *Ecological Economics* 35.
26 See Huguenin, Donlan, van Geel and Paterson, 'Assessment and Valuation of Damage to the Environment', op cit, 78.
27 Ibid., 80.
28 See US Office of Management and Budget, Circular A-4, *Guidance on Development of Regulatory Analysis* (2003); US Environmental Protection Agency, *Guidelines for Preparing Economic Analyses* (2000).
29 Yang, Telesetsky, Harmon-Walker and Percival, *Comparative and Global Environmental Law and Policy*, op cit, 299.
30 INECE, *Principles of Environmental Compliance and Enforement Handbook: Creating Value Through Compliance* (April 2009).
31 Yang, Telesetsky, Harmon-Walker and Percival, *Comparative and Global Environmental Law and Policy*, op cit, 311.
32 Peter Wetterstein, 'A Proprietary or Possessory Interest: A Conditio Sine Qua Non for Claiming Damages for Environmental Impairment?' in Peter Wetterstein (ed.), *Harm to the Environment: The Right to Compensation and the Assessment of Damages* (Clarendon Press, 1997), 33.
33 See, e.g., *In re Oil Spill by Amoco Cadiz Off Coast of France on March 16, 1978*, 954 F.2d 1279 (7th Cir. 1992).
34 Ibid.
35 Ibid.
36 Paul Portney, 'The Contingent Valuation Debate: Why Economists Should Care' 8(4) (1994) *Journal of Economic Perspectives* 3.
37 Ibid.
38 See also Report on the Activities of the International Oil Pollution Compensation Fund During 1978 and 1979, https://iopcfunds.org/wp-content/uploads/2018/12/1978___1979_ANNUAL_REPORT.pdf.
39 IOPC, Resolution No. 3 – Pollution Damage (October 1980).

40 *Patmos Case*, Court of Appeal Messina (24 December 1993), 4 IELR 288. See also, IOPC Doc. FUND/Exc.30/2, para 4.15 (29 November 1991); Andrea Bianchi, 'Harm to the Environment in Italian Practice: The Interaction of International Law and Domestic Law' in Wetterstein (ed.), *Harm to the Environment: The Right to Compensation and the Assessment of Damages*, op cit, 103.
41 IOPC Funds, *Annual Report* (1999), 42–8.
42 *Commonwealth of Puerto Rico v. The MV Zoe Colocotroni*, 628 F.2d 652 (1st Cir. 1980), 675.
43 Ibid.
44 Ibid.
45 *State of Ohio v. Department of the Interior* 880 F. 2d 432 (DC Cir 1989).
46 Ibid., 464.
47 Nick Hanley, 'The Economic Value of Environmental Damage' in Bowman and Boyle (eds.), *Environmental Damage in International and Comparative Law*, op cit, 34.
48 Ibid.
49 Ibid., 35.
50 *Erika Case*, Arrêt No. 3439, Cour de Cassation (25 September 2012).
51 Yang, Telesetsky, Harmon-Walker and Percival, *Comparative and Global Environmental Law and Policy*, op cit, 314.
52 *VIGIPOL et autres v. Totalfina et autres*, Tribunal de Grand Instance de Paris, 4eme session (2008).
53 Yang, Telesetsky, Harmon-Walker and Percival, *Comparative and Global Environmental Law and Policy*, op cit, 314.
54 See Biodiversity Law No. 2016–1087 of 8 August 2016.
55 Translation provided in Yang, Telesetsky, Harmon-Walker and Percival, *Comparative and Global Environmental Law and Policy*, op cit, 314.
56 See Peter Wetterstein, 'Environmental Damage in the Legal Systems of the Nordic Countries and Germany', in Bowman and Boyle (eds.), *Environmental Damage in International and Comparative Law*, op cit, 241.
57 Supreme Court of Sweden (1995) NJA 249.
58 Wetterstein, 'The Nordic Countries and Germany', op cit, 241.
59 2013 Swedish Governmental Investigation on Ecosystem Services (SOU 2013:168).
60 The litigation included *In re: Oil Spill By the Oil Rig 'Deepwater Horizon' in the Gulf of Mexico, on April 20, 2010* United States District Court, Eastern District Louisiana, 2010 MDL No. 2179 (2011).
61 Ron Bousso, 'BP Deepwater Horizon Costs Balloon to $65 Billion', *Reuters*, 16 January 2018, www.reuters.com/article/us-bp-deepwaterhorizon/bp-deepwater-horizon-costs-balloon-to-65-billion-idUSKBN1F50NL.
62 National Oceanic and Atmospheric Administration, 'Deepwater Horizon Oil Spill Settlements: Where the Money Went', www.noaa.gov/explainers/deepwater-horizon-oil-spill-settlements-where-money-went.
63 See George Pring and Katherine Pring, 'Greening Justice: Creating and Improving Environmental Courts and Tribunals', *The Access Initiative Report*, 2009, www.eufje.org/images/DocDivers/Rapport%20Pring.pdf.
64 Brian Preston, 'Characteristics of Successful Environmental Courts and Tribunals' 26 (2014) *Journal of Environmental Law* 365.
65 Ibid.

66 Alana Marsili, 'A New Court in Guatemala Tackles Ecoside', *FrontLines* (2015), www.usaid.gov/news-information/frontlines/resilience-2015/new-court-guatemala-tackles-ecocide.

67 For a good overview, see United Nations Environment Programme, *The Status of Climate Litigation: A Global Review* (UN Environment and Columbia Law School, 2017); Margaretha Wewerinke-Singh, *State Responsibility, Climate Change and Human Rights under International Law* (Hart, 2019).

68 See, for example, *Massachusetts v. EPA* 549 US 497 (2007).

69 See, for example, *Am. Elec. Power Co. v. Connecticut* 564 US 410 (2011); *Native Vill. of Kivalina v. ExxonMobil Corp.* 696 F.3d 849 (9th Cir. 2012).

70 See, for example, *Juliana v. United States*, No. 6:15-cv-1517-TC, 2016 WL 183903 (D. Or. Jan. 14, 2016). The federal appeals courts ruled in favour of 21 teenagers suing the US government for its energy and climate change policies.

71 See, for example, *Friends of the Earth v. Canada* [2008] F.C. 1183 (Can. Fed. Ct.).

72 See, for example, *Leghari v. Fedn. of Pakistan*, W.P. No. 25501/2015 (Lahore High Court) (4 September 2015).

73 See, for example, *Gbemre v. Shell Petroleum Dev. Co. Nigeria* [2005] Afr. Hum. Rts. L. Rep. 151

74 See, for example, *Greenpeace New Zealand v. Northland Reg'l Council* [2006] NZHC CIV 2006–404–004617; *Genesis Power Ltd. v. Franklin Dist. Council* [2005] NZRMA 541.

75 *The Netherlands v. Urgenda*, No. 200.178.245/01 (2018). The case has been upheld by the Hague Court of Appeal on 9 October 2018.

76 Ibid.

77 See, for example, Case C-366/10 *Air Transport of America et al v. Secretary of State for Energy and Climate Change* (Grand Chamber) [2001] ECR II-864.

78 *The People's Climate Case (Armando Ferrão Carvalho and Others v. European Parliament and Council)*, No. T-330/18.

79 People's Climate Case, 'Families affected by the climate case file appeal after the European General Court dismisses their case', https://peoplesclimatecase. caneurope.org/2019/07/families-affected-by-the-climate-crisis-file-appeal-after-the-european-general-court-dismisses-their-case/.

80 Ibid.

81 Ibid.

5 Economic and philosophical approaches to valuing environmental damage

Introduction

This chapter considers various environmental damage valuation techniques that have emerged from the assessment of the different regimes in the previous chapters, as well as others that environmental economists and philosophers have developed. In many cases, judges and arbitrators have relied exclusively on what economists call direct use value.[1] This value has significant blind spots and often fails to account for environmental damage in its entirety, such as a diminution in carbon sequestration or of watershed protection offered by the natural environment. Alternatively, many valuation approaches can have a sub-optimal deterrence effect. While some courts have insisted that punitive compensation is not permitted under international law,[2] other international tribunals have nevertheless awarded relief that reflects the egregious behaviour of a party.[3] The ILC's Commentary to the Draft Articles on State Responsibility note that 'environmental damage will often extend beyond that which can be readily quantified in terms of clean-up costs or property devaluation'.[4] Indeed, the ILC envisaged that compensation could be awarded for damage caused beyond the expenses incurred in preventing or remedying pollution – for example – or in lieu of the reduced value of property that may result from pollution.

Moreover, courts and tribunals, particularly human rights courts, have a wealth of experience in awarding compensation with respect to non-material damage, which may also be referred to as moral damage in many national legal systems. Such damage may include the loss of a relative, pain and suffering, the distress caused by an intrusion on the person or someone's home. Non-material damage may also be financially assessed, as was illustrated by the *Lusitania* and *M/V Saiga* cases referred to in Chapter 1, where personal injury and loss were compensated and the *López Ostra v. Spain* case of the European Court of Human Rights in Chapter 2. We will turn now to consider the various methods developed by economists and philosophers, some of which take a broader range of values into account.

Economic valuation of the environment

The economic value of environmental goods can be divided into use values and non-use values. As for use values, these can include direct use values, indirect use values or option values. First, direct use values compromise economic utility to individuals. These are goods or services consumed directly or indirectly in production processes or experience value. In other words, individuals either consume an environmental good or service (e.g., as water for drinking, meat or vegetables for eating, wood for furniture, etc.) or experience it (e.g., hiking in nature, bird watching, etc.). Second, indirect use values include the functional value or ecosystem services rendered by the environment. As such, society derives benefits from the functions of the ecosystem (e.g., as carbon sequestration, flood control, storm protection, etc.). Third, option values are the potential future use of the environment. This is the amount people are willing to pay for the option of using a resource in the future (e.g., a future visit to a national park, potential pharmaceutical uses of natural resources, etc.).[5]

Non-use values, on the other hand, may comprise existence values, altruistic values or bequest values. First, existence values reflect the utility derived from knowing the natural environment exists and is protected. This is determined by individuals' willingness to pay to keep a resource for the sake of its existence, rather than for any consumption or experience they may desire from it. Second, bequest value is the utility derived from knowing that the environment will be preserved for future generations. Third, altruistic value is the utility in the knowledge that natural goods may be available for others in the present generation to enjoy.[6]

Use and non-use values must be derived from the affected population. Given that some people may be affected positively and some negatively by a given change to the environment, these values must be aggregated. Total economic value is given by the sum of both use and non-use values.[7]

Economists often measure environmental change, whether that be an improvement or a diminution, by assessing the preferences of individuals for that change. The concepts of 'maximum willingness to pay' (WTP) and 'minimum willingness to accept compensation' (WTAC) are used to assess changes in environmental quality. As such, people's WTP to implement an improvement or avoid a diminution in environmental quality is calculated by reference to the level of goods, services or money individuals are willing to sacrifice to implement or avoid the environmental change.[8] Alternatively, individual preferences can be appraised by determining individuals' WTAC to forgo the improvement in the environment or to endure the diminution. This is the level of goods, services or money people will accept to forgo or put up with the environmental change.[9] It is much like the valuation of a rare painting, whose value is determined by the most anyone is willing to pay for it.[10] In the context of the environment, if an area of woodland is planned to be felled, the value is given by the maximum those living nearby are willing to pay to keep the woodland or the minimum amount they are willing to accept in compensation for it to be felled.[11]

Economists can use markets to determine WTP and WTAC by observing consumption and production behaviour among buyers and sellers. The fluctuation in market price can thus give the WTP or WTAC values. For certain environmental goods and services, WTP can be calculated from the value of those resources on the commercial market. However, many environmental goods and services are not traded in a commercial market. As such, preferences and value (i.e., WTP and WTAC) have to be determined differently.

As is becoming evident, these valuations are anthropocentric and focused on the value or utility the environment delivers to human beings. Some have considered that other conceptions of environmental value, such as the intrinsic value of the environment, should be taken into consideration. We will return to this later in the chapter. As most valuation techniques are to a greater or lesser extent based on the anthropocentric value categories set out earlier, we will first explore the methods that are used to determine these values.

Economic valuation techniques

Economic valuation techniques can themselves be grouped into three categories for the purposes of explanation. These include conventional market techniques, revealed preference techniques or stated preference techniques. First, conventional market techniques are concerned with observable market prices to measure the value of something. They are typically used where environmental damage has an impact on commerce that is connected with the natural resources damaged. It is limited to determining the use values of goods or services available on the market, and the value is derived from the market price of a produce (minus taxes or subsidies that may have been levied). Second, revealed preference techniques rely on the discovery of surrogate markets for environmental goods and services. The value of those goods and services are determined by reference to the price of other goods and services (e.g., travel costs to visit a natural resource). They provide an estimate of environmental value. Third, stated preference techniques use surveys to construct hypothetical markets. Through these surveys, individuals state their preferences. Unlike many other economic valuation methods, stated preference techniques can be used to estimate both use and non-use values. Indeed, it is important to point out that, in the context of environmental resources, non-use values can constitute a large part of total economic value.[12] This is particularly the case where the environmental resource is unique or the damage to it is irreversible.

Stated preference approaches

In stated preference techniques, questionnaires or surveys are conducted to assess individuals' preferences. Stated preference techniques can include contingent valuation – which is concerned with assessing WTP or WTAC through surveys – or choice modelling, which is concerned with assessing preferences from a range of alternative choices given to respondents in a survey. As we are most interested in valuation techniques, we will consider contingent valuation only.

Contingent valuation

Contingent valuation is the most used stated preference approach. It is a direct valuation method and typically involves a survey of willingness to pay more tax to invest in environmental goods. Participants may be asked how much they are WTP or WTAC through open or closed questions. This approach would, for example, ask a random group of people in Portugal how much they might be willing to pay to prevent oil spills in the Atlantic Ocean. Econometric means are then used to calculate the average WTP or WTAC value from the survey results. The valuation of the environmental resource is thus determined on the basis of a community's WTP or WTAC.

It can be used for all cost and utility categories, such as noise abatement measures, individual disutility due to health risks, reduced life expectancy or willingness to pay for the preservation of biodiversity. Moreover, it can be used to estimate both use and non-use values. Further still, it does not require any precedential data to give an estimate of value. However, there is concern over how accurate valuation estimates are since they rely on hypothetical commitments rather than real behaviour. Indeed, some economists critique this approach as they argue that stated preferences can be unreliable given the multitude of factors that can vary perceptions of environmental goods.[13] It can also be expensive to conduct given the original data collection that is required by the approach.

This was proposed by certain parties in the context of the UNCC, although the UNCC ultimately did not adopt the approach. In the context of the UNCC, Kuwait claimed lost recreational activities at the beach as a result of Iraq's invasion of Kuwait. The value of these lost recreational activities was calculated using contingent valuation. As such, surveys about the recreational activities of individuals had been conducted 10 years after Iraq's invasion. The F4 Panel was concerned that these surveys were not reliable because of the length of time that had elapsed since the original event. Given the unreliability of the information gathered from the surveys and other factors, the F4 Panel recommended that no award be made in respect of this claim.[14] It has, however, been used in the US to determine damage to natural resources.[15]

Revealed preference techniques

In revealed preference techniques, economic values are determined by observing actual changes in behaviour in related markets.[16] WTP information is derived from the preferences that individuals make in actual markets. In the context of environmental goods or services, revealed preference techniques can only estimate use values. They can indicate, for example, the use value of a natural resource for recreation or of fish for commercial sale. As such, they do not indicate non-use value and therefore fail to give an estimate of total economic value on their own.

Travel cost method

A common approach is the travel cost method. It assesses how much people pay to use environmental goods or places, and as a result it reveals the recreational value. It can include transport fares, fuel costs, wear and tear, expenses such as entry costs and value of time spent, amongst other factors. As such, it is known as an indirect valuation method. It is typically based on data that exists, rather than on the conduct of a survey specifically gathering data for the purpose of valuing environmental change. Usually, the amount people are WTP in petrol or on train tickets reveals something about the value of the place they visit. Where the quality of an environment deteriorates, the amount people are willing to pay to visit it will similarly decrease.

Its principal advantage lies in the fact that it uses real market data. It can be particularly useful in estimating the recreation value of national parks, reservoirs, woodlands, forests or wetlands, for example. That said, this approach has a number of disadvantages. For example, it does not capture non-use values, as it is based on the visits people actually make to a location. Consequently, this valuation technique may not reflect the total economic value of the environment concerned.[17] Moreover, it presents problems with respect to multi-purpose trips, valuing travel and leisure time, and it requires precedent to predict changes in use values that result from environmental degradation.[18]

Hedonic pricing method

Hedonic pricing is another revealed preference approach. It relies on an assessment of statistical relationships between environmental quality levels and marketed goods.[19] It is, as such, an indirect valuation method. Hedonic pricing could include, for example, an assessment of the influence of environmental quality on the housing market. The value of property is likely to fall where air quality deteriorates, noise increases or the landscape or water quality degrades.[20] Concretely, it has been used to estimate decreases in the value of property where waste disposal sites have been located in the vicinity,[21] the economic costs of noise pollution[22] or the economic value of planting forests.[23]

As with the travel costs method, this approach uses real market data to give estimates of value. However, as a result, the approach can only give estimates of use values, and it does not indicate estimates of non-use values. It also requires a significant amount of housing market data and requires a precedent to predict changes in value.

Avertive or avoided expenditure approach

The avertive expenditure approach reveals how much individuals are WTP to circumvent the consequences of environmental degradation. For example, people may buy a water filter where water quality deteriorates or insert double-glazing to reduce the impact of noise. The price paid for these measures is taken to indicate the loss of utility in an environmental change.[24] It is most useful in assessing environmental value in the context of water quality, noise abatement or air pollution, for example. The approach uses real market data and does not require significant amounts of data to provide estimates. However, it can only indicate use values and presents problems where there are multiple reasons why people purchase a good that is characterised as an avertive measure (e.g., double-glazing may insulate against noise, but it can also insulate against the cold).[25]

Benefits transfer techniques

A benefits transfer approach involves taking values estimated for other similar resources and adjusting them to accord with local circumstances. The benefits of one site (known as the 'study site') are applied to another site (known as the 'policy site').[26] It has the potential to reduce the amount of primary or original information that must be gathered in a given valuation exercise, thus making the exercise more efficient. It is of course limited by the extent to which the data from the study site fits the characteristics of the policy site. This can lead to a wide margin for inaccuracy.

The basic requirements of a benefits transfer approach have been identified in economic literature. First, the original studies must be sound. Second, the studies need to show how WTP or WTAC varies under different conditions. Third, there should be sufficient similarity between the study and policy sites, particularly as to population and site characteristics. Where differences exist, these should be adjusted for. Fourth, the change at both sites should be similar. Fifth, either WTP or WTAC should be used as a measure consistently at both sites, rather than using WTP for one site and WTAC for the other or vice versa. Finally, property rights ought to be similar at the different sites.[27]

As was evident in the previous chapter, a benefits transfer was conducted in the *American Trader* litigation with respect to lost beach days. It has also been used in the context of the UNCC. In that context, for example, Iran conducted a benefits transfer by applying resource values estimated by a previous study to estimate losses with respect to rangelands that had been damaged by the livestock of refugees. However, the environmental panel of the UNCC was not convinced that the value estimates were transferable given that there were significant differences in the location and subject matter of the previous study. Nevertheless, the panel was able to use some of the values put forward by Iran from the study, namely the cost of replacement fodder, to make a partial award.[28]

Restoration cost method

The restoration cost method values damage to the environment by reference to the cost incurred in its restoration. It is an approach that is used often given the relative ease with which such restoration costs can be determined by reference to the expenditure required to restore the environment. Such values can be indicated by actual costs or professional estimates. As was evident in previous chapters, this approach is regularly used in giving the value of oil clean-up operations. However, it does not give the value (total economic value or otherwise) of the environment per se but rather the cost of restoring it. As such, it potentially underestimates total economic value because some damage may not be recognised or restored.[29]

Analysis of economic techniques

The methods that rely on stated or revealed preferences have been the subject of critique for various reasons. First, some have argued that approaches relying on human satisfaction do not take into account the value of ecosystems.[30] The value of ecosystems is evidently more difficult to measure in monetary terms than it is to measure market or non-market goods that are consumed by human beings. We will return to methods that do take account of the value of ecosystems later. Second, there are sometimes concerns about the accuracy of stated and revealed preference approaches. For example, there is likely to be a difference between WTP and WTAC valuations. WTP is closely linked to income and thus is likely to vary depending on income levels. Moreover, people tend to value losses much more highly than equivalent gains. This is known in behavioural economics as loss aversion, which is disproportionately more powerful than equivalent gain satisfaction.[31]

Nevertheless, WTP and WTAC techniques can be helpful in determining value where no market value exists for a given resource or quality of environment. Many environmental goods are in fact so-called non-market goods, that is they are not valued by the market.[32] As such, when an oil spill occurs on the coastline, the market does not give a value for beach days, sea gulls and otters since they are not bought and sold on the market. While they are non-market goods, they can still have economic value.

More generally, the problems with the various valuation techniques set out previously can include the robustness of value estimates, the aggregation procedure and the transferability of estimates. The robustness of value estimates is affected, for example, by choices made by statisticians or the design of studies or surveys, particularly the amount of information given to participants.[33] Moreover, contingent valuation relies on hypothetical commitments rather than actual behaviour.[34] Often real WTP can be much lower than stated WTP, though economists have differed on the extent to which this may occur and variation may depend on the kind of environmental damage at issue as well as the design of the contingent study.[35] The transferability of estimates in relation to benefits transfer approaches has been shown in some situations to present accuracy problems.[36] This might be the case particularly when benefits transfer methods are made between different countries or for very different circumstances.

The restoration cost method is based on the cost of replacing or restoring an environmental resource, and some economists are sceptical of this method as a valuation technique. First, it does not express preferences but rather costs. Second, it may be that full restoration of the environment is not possible, and therefore it underestimates the value of the damage. Third, it ignores many other elements of disutility, such as the time that restoration can take or the psychological costs that may result from environmental damage.

We turn now to consider valuation concepts that take into account a broader range of values provided by the environment, addressing some of the concerns that have been raised in respect of the previous methods.

Intrinsic value of the environment

While economic conceptions of the value of the environment may be much broader than we initially think them to be, particularly encompassing as they can market and non-market values, they are also based squarely on an anthropocentric view of nature. Total economic value may or may not reflect the intrinsic value of the environment as intrinsic value can have a greater or lesser impact on WTP or WTAC.[37] Some valuation techniques may capture intrinsic value better than others.[38] Intrinsic value does not involve assigning market values but is rather an expression that entities like the environment have value in and of themselves.[39]

Three broad notions of value have been identified by scholars. These are instrumental, inherent and intrinsic value.[40] First, instrumental value is derived from the practical utility that the entity serves. This is most easily calculated by the economic value that an entity has (e.g., how much fish costs as food). It is also referred to as use value.[41] Second, inherent value, on the other hand, is concerned with the value an entity has for its very existence, rather than its utility (e.g., this may be the value accorded for the enjoyment or aesthetic appeal of the environment).[42] Third, intrinsic value does not depend on any external valuation by human beings, but rather it is based on the notion that goods can have a value in and of themselves and for themselves. This kind of value does not depend on economic actors but nevertheless deserves to be taken into our moral consideration.[43]

While calculating the loss of intrinsic value may be complex, certain methods have been suggested. Alder and Wilkinson, for example, have observed that '[t]here is room within the economic approach for concerns about the intrinsic value of nature for its own sake since economic evaluation depends on human preferences'.[44] The valuation frameworks discussed later take intrinsic value into account better than those discussed earlier in isolation.

There are also many references to intrinsic value in conventional practice. The 1980 World Charter for Nature sets out in its Preamble that 'every form of life is unique, warranting respect regardless of its worth to man'. The Bern Convention on the Conservation of European Wildlife and Natural Habitats of 1979 notes that fauna and flora 'constitute a natural heritage of aesthetic, scientific, cultural, recreational, economic and intrinsic value'. The Convention on Biodiversity recognises in its Preamble the 'intrinsic value of biological diversity', as well as recognizing separately the various forms of instrumental and inherent value delivered by biological diversity. Moreover, the Convention on International Trade in Endangered Species (CITES) contains many references to the importance of conserving species as well as ensuring the welfare of individual organisms. The 1991 Protocol to the Antarctic Treaty provides in Article 2 for the 'intrinsic value of Antarctica'. Though it has been observed that the Antarctic Environmental Protocol goes on to stipulate that such intrinsic value includes 'its wilderness and aesthetic values and its values as an area for the conduct of scientific research', which appears to confuse intrinsic value with the notions of inherent and instrumental value.[45] That said, it has also been suggested that this highlights how 'intrinsic value is the primary form of value from which all others derive'.[46] Many agree that individual organisms, species, ecosystems and the biosphere all have intrinsic value because they are self-realising, they define their own self-interest, and what happens to them matters because they are always attempting to preserve their own integrity and identity.[47]

The interconnected nature of ecosystems has been observed by scholars. While an ecosystem is made up of independent organisms, their existence depends on other elements in the ecosystem. Indeed, it has been said that

> An ecosystem generates a spontaneous order that envelops and produces the richness, beauty, integrity and dynamic stability of the component parts. Though these organized interdependencies are loose in comparison with the tight connections within an organism, all these metabolisms are as vitally linked as are liver and heart. The equilibrating ecosystem is not merely push-pull forces. It is equilibrating of values.[48]

No other intrinsic values could exist in nature without the ecosystem.[49] While it may be challenging to appraise the monetary value of losing intrinsic value, this should be no more difficult than awarding compensation for the pain and suffering in human injury that results from unlawful behaviour.[50] Tariff systems that classify amounts for certain types of damage have been suggested, as has the idea that where reparation for such loss is not possible, compensation should be paid to an environmental fund that assists with other natural conservation work.[51] It seems appropriate and possible, therefore, that compensation can be calculated by having regard for the loss of biological diversity or damage to ecosystems.

Techniques that account for such value might better serve the preservation of a resource or the environment in general. Methodologies that encompass broader notions of damage will certainly be more appropriate for calculating compensation for harm caused by climate change. Given the growing wave of national and regional climate litigation,[52] it is only a matter of time before an international tribunal has to adjudicate a case of this kind.

We now turn to consider specific valuation frameworks that take into account these broader concerns about intrinsic or ecosystem value.

Habitat and resource equivalency analysis

Habitat and resource equivalency analyses (HEA and REA respectively) have been used more frequently in recent years. Indeed, they have seen application in US and EU practice.[53] HEA and REA estimate the ecological value of environmental damage by assessing the amount of resources required to compensate for losses in ecosystem services. They thus give a more complex picture of environmental damage by emphasizing the impairment of the many ecological services provided by the environment and highlight the full restoration of those services rather than just the services that the environment provides directly to human beings. Both HEA and REA rely on biological and toxicological data. They assess the exposure of a given resource to a toxicant and extrapolate the scale of injury that is consistent with that exposure.[54] In HEA, the biological, physical and chemical elements of a habitat provide a given number of natural resource service units. These units are called Service Acre Years (SAYs). This unit is the level of natural resource service collectively provided by an acre of the habitat. HEA is particularly suitable for projects involving restoration of the environment.

As noted in Chapter 3, HEA was used in the context of some claims before the UNCC. Indeed, the HEA valuation technique was applied to Saudi Arabia's claim regarding its polluted shoreline. The F4 Panel decided that two marine and coastal preserves could replace the outstanding ecosystem services and recommended that compensation of USD46.1 million be paid.[55] This HEA valuation technique was used in respect of other claims as well. For example, in Jordan's claim regarding damaged rangeland and wildlife reserves that had been caused by traffic, overgrazing by the livestock of refugees and the plants that refuges had yielded for fuel and Kuwait's claim that ecological services in its desert had been damaged by tarcrete, windblown sand, oil pollution, fortifications and ordnance.[56]

REA is similar in approach but differs in its precise application compared with HEA. The environmental damage to specific resources is instead considered. As such, resource specific units are used to quantify the damage to the concerned resource (e.g., bird year).[57] It is very data-intensive since a great deal of information on life-history, reproductive capacity, population density and others are required for the assessment of biological resources, while a similarly wide range of data sets are required for the assessment of non-biological resources.[58] For both HEA and REA approaches data can be site-specific or extrapolated from published literature.

Ecosystem services approach

Ecosystem services are defined as 'the benefits provided by ecosystems to humans that contribute to making human life both possible and worth living'.[59] The Conceptual Framework Working Group of the Millennium Ecosystem Assessment published a framework for an ecosystem services approach to assessing environmental damage in their 2003 report 'Ecosystems and Human Well-being: A Framework for Assessment', which has been authored by various UN and other actors.[60] Ecosystem services include provisioning services (e.g., food and water), regulating services (e.g., flood, drought, land degradation, climate change and disease prevention), supporting services (e.g., soil formation and nutrient cycling) and cultural services (e.g., recreational, spiritual, religious and other non-material benefits).[61] This analytical framework for assessing environmental damage is therefore very comprehensive. Once the damage has been assessed, depending on the ecosystem service being valued, combinations of the previously mentioned valuation techniques or other value transfer methods can be used to give a valuation of compensation due.

Several organisations have emphasised the importance of an ecosystems approach. For example, the United Nations Environment Programme, the World Resources Institute and the European Commission have all set up initiatives or published reports and guidelines on the valuation of ecosystem services.[62] It has been suggested that the ecosystem services approach may provide a more accurate picture in large-scale complex restoration projects where HEA or REA may oversimplify the task of calculating the value of environmental damage.[63]

Concluding remarks

A more complex understanding of the environment can help to reveal the values of the environment that would otherwise remain hidden. For example, where a damaged area is reduced in its capacity for carbon sequestration, it would be appropriate to take measures to restore that capacity as soon as possible, even if this means taking measures to offset carbon emissions while the affected area is being restored to its original state. Similarly, lost trees may affect the air quality in the area, which can in turn create public health problems and, therefore, increase costs. It may be necessary to ensure that additional measures are taken to maintain air quality levels while the original site is being restored. An ecosystem services approach to environmental damage assessment and valuation can ensure that provisioning and other services provided by ecosystems do not go unnoticed. This framework, used in combination with the variety of methods discussed in this chapter, can help to give a full picture of environmental damage.

Notes

1 See, for example, *Certain Activities Carried Out By Nicaragua in the Border Area (Costa Rica v. Nicaragua) (Compensation)*, ICJ General List No. 150 (2 February 2018); *Burlington Resources v. Ecuador*, ICSID Case No. ARB/ 08/5, Decision on Ecuador's Counterclaim (7 February 2017); *Perenco v. Ecuador and Empresa Estatal Petróleos del Ecuador (Petroecuador)*, ICSID Case No. ARB/08/6, Interim Decision on the Environmental Counterclaim (11 August 2015).
2 *Costa Rica v. Nicaragua (Compensation)*, para 31.
3 See, e.g., *I'm Alone Case*, III (1933–1935) Reports of International Arbitral Awards 1609; *Rainbow Warrior Affair*, XX (1990) Reports of International Arbitral Awards 215; *Eritrea-Ethiopia Claims Commission*, Final Award, 26 [2009] Reports of International Arbitral Awards 631, paras 103, 310–12.
4 Draft Articles on the Responsibility of States for Internationally Wrongful Acts II(2) YBILC (2001), 101.
5 European Commission – Directorate-General Environment, *Study on the Valuation and Restoration of Biodiversity Damage for the Purpose of Environmental Liability* (B4–3040/2000/265781/MAR/B3) (May 2001), 2.
6 See Sylvia Schwermer, *Economic Valuation of Environmental Damage: Methodological Convention 2.0 for Estimates of Environmental Costs* (Umwelt Bundesamt, 2012). Davis Pearce and Dominic Moran, 'The Economics of Biological Diversity Conservation' in Peggy Fiedler and Peter Kareiva (eds.) *Conservation Biology: For the Coming Decade* (Chapman and Hall, 1998), 384–409.
7 European Commission – Directorate-General Environment, *Study on the Valuation and Restoration of Biodiversity Damage for the Purpose of Environmental Liability*, op cit, 2.
8 Ibid., 1.
9 Ibid.
10 Nick Hanley, 'The Economic Value of Environmental Damage' in Michael Bowman and Alan Boyle (eds.), *Environmental Damage in International and Comparative Law: Problems of Definition and Valuation* (Oxford University Press, 2001), 28.
11 Ibid.
12 Ibid., 4.
13 See, for example, Peter Diamond and Jerry Hausman, 'Contingent Valuation: Is Some Number Better Than No Number?' (1994) *Journal of Economic Perspectives* 45, 56, 63.
14 Michael Huguenin, Michael Donlan, Alexandra van Geel and Robert Paterson, 'Assessment and Valuation of Damage to the Environment' in Cymie R. Payne and Peter H. Sand (eds.), *Gulf War Reparations and the UN Compensation Commission* (Oxford University Press, 2011), 90–1; See also UNCC, *Report and Recommendations Made By the Panel of Commissioners Concerning the Fifth Instalment of 'F4' Claims* (30 June 2005), UN Doc. S/AC.26/2005/10, paras 462–4.
15 Daniel Farber, 'The UNCC as a Model for Climate Compensation' in Payne and Sand (eds.), *Gulf War Reparations and the UN Compensation Commission*, op cit, 251.

16 Hanley, 'The Economic Value of Environmental Damage', op cit, 31.
17 Ibid., 32.
18 European Commission – Directorate-General Environment, *Study on the Valuation and Restoration of Biodiversity Damage for the Purpose of Environmental Liability*, op cit, 7.
19 Ibid., 7.
20 Ibid.
21 Stephen Farber, 'Undesirable Facilities and Property Values: A Summary of Empirical Studies' 24(1) (1998) *Ecological Economics* 1.
22 Ian Bateman, Brett Day, Iain Lake and Andrew Lovett, *The Effect of Road Traffic on Residential Property Values*, Final Report to the Scottish Executive (January 2001), www.webarchive.org.uk/wayback/archive/20170701074158/www.gov.scot/Publications/2001/07/9535.
23 Guy Garrod and Ken Willis, 'The Amenity Value of Woodland in Great Britain' 2(4) (1992) *Environmental and Resource Economics* 415.
24 European Commission – Directorate-General Environment, *Study on the Valuation and Restoration of Biodiversity Damage for the Purpose of Environmental Liability*, op cit, 8.
25 Ibid.
26 Ibid., 5.
27 Ibid., 13.
28 Huguenin, Donlan, van Geel and Paterson, 'Assessment and Valuation of Damage to the Environment', op cit, 90; *Report and Recommendations Made By the Panel of Commissioners Concerning the Fifth Instalment of 'F4' Claims*, op cit, 39.
29 European Commission – Directorate-General Environment, *Study on the Valuation and Restoration of Biodiversity Damage for the Purpose of Environmental Liability*, op cit, 9.
30 Hanley, 'The Economic Value of Environmental Damage', op cit, 33.
31 Daniel Kahneman and Amos Tversky, 'Prospect Theory: An Analysis of Decision under Risk' 47(4) (1979) *Econometrica* 263.
32 Nick Hanley, Jason Shogren and Ben White, *An Introduction to Environmental Economics* (Oxford University Press, 2001).
33 Alistair Munro and Nick Hanley, 'Information, Uncertainty and Contingent Valuation' in Ian Bateman and Ken Willis (eds.), *Valuation of Environmental Preferences: Theory and Practice of the Contingent Valuation Method in the US, EU and Developing Countries* (Oxford University Press, 2001); Ian Bateman, Ian Langford and Jon Rasbash, 'Willingness-to-Pay Question Format Effects in Contingent Valuation Studies' in Bateman and Willis (eds.), *Valuation of Environmental Preferences: Theory and Practice of the Contingent Valuation Method in the US, EU and Developing Countries*, op cit.
34 Jerry Hausman, *Contingent Valuation: A Critical Assessment* (Emerald Publishing, 1993).
35 Peter Frikblom, 'Hypothetical Question Modes and Real Willingness to Pay' 34(3) (1997) *Journal of Environmental Economics and Management* 275; Vivien Foster, Ian Bateman and David Harley, 'Real versus Hypothetical Willingness to Pay for Environmental Protection' 48(2) (1997) *Journal of Agricultural Economics* 123.
36 Olvar Bergland, Kristin Magnussen and Stale Navrud, 'Benefit Transfer: Testing for Accuracy and Reliability' in Raymond Florax, Peter Nijkamp, and Kenneth Willis (eds.), *Comparative Environmental Economic Assessment: Meta Analysis and Benefit Transfer* (Elgar, 1999).

37 European Commission – Directorate-General Environment, *Study on the Valuation and Restoration of Biodiversity Damage for the Purpose of Environmental Liability*, op cit, 2.
38 Ibid.
39 Robin Attfield, *The Ethics of Environmental Concern* (University of Georgia Press, 1991); Freya Mathews, *The Ecological Self* (Routledge, 1991); Michael Bowman, 'Biodiversity, Intrinsic Value, and the Definition and Valuation of Environmental Harm' in Bowman and Boyle (eds.), *Environmental Damage in International and Comparative Law*, op cit; *Costa Rica v. Nicaragua (Compensation)*, Dissenting Opinion of Judge *Ad Hoc* Dugard, para 29.
40 Attfield, *The Ethics of Environmental Concern*, op cit; Mathews, *The Ecological Self*, op cit; Bowman, 'Biodiversity, Intrinsic Value, and the Definition and Valuation of Environmental Harm', op cit.
41 Bowman, 'Biodiversity, Intrinsic Value, and the Definition and Valuation of Environmental Harm', op cit, 45.
42 Ibid.; M. Flint, 'Biological Diversity and Developing Countries' in Anil Markandya and Julie Richardson (eds.), *Earthscan Reader in Environmental Economics* (Taylor and Francis, 1992), 441.
43 Mathews, *The Ecological Self*, op cit, 118.
44 John Alder and David Wilkinson, *Environmental Law and Ethics* (Springer, 1999).
45 Bowman, 'Biodiversity, Intrinsic Value, and Harm', op cit, 47.
46 Ibid.
47 Mathews, *The Ecological Self*, op cit.
48 Holmes Rolston, *Conserving Natural Value* (Columbia University Press, 1994), 23.
49 Ibid., 24.
50 Bowman, 'Biodiversity, Intrinsic Value, and Harm', op cit, 59.
51 Ibid., 60.
52 See, e.g., *The Netherlands v. Urgenda*, No. 200.178.245/01 (2018); *Juliana v. United States*, No. 6:15-cv-1517-TC (2016); *Air Transport of America et al v. Secretary of State for Energy and Climate Change* [2001] ECR II-864; *People's Climate Case (Armando Ferrão Carvalho and Others v. European Parliament and Council*, No. T-330/18.
53 William Desvousges, Nicholas Gard, Holly Michael and Anne Chance, 'Habitat and Resource Equivalency Analysis: A Critical Assessment' 143 (2018) *Ecological Economics* 74.
54 Lawrence Barnthouse and Ralph Stahl, 'Assessing and Managing Natural Resource Damages: Continuing Challenges and Opportunities' 59 (2017) *Environmental Management* 709, 712.
55 *Report and Recommendations Made By the Panel of Commissioners Concerning the Fifth Instalment of 'F4' Claims*, op cit, paras 611–36.
56 Ibid., paras 362–3 and 413–75.
57 Barnthouse and Stahl, 'Assessing and Managing Natural Resource Damages: Continuing Challenges and Opportunities', op cit, 713.
58 Ibid.
59 National Research Council and Committee on the Effects of the Deepwater Horizon Mississippi Canon-252 Oil Spill on Ecosystem Services in the Gulf of Mexico; Ocean Studies Board; Division on Earth and Life Sciences, 2013, 2.
60 Conceptual Framework Working Group of the Millennium Ecosystem Assessment, *Ecosystems and Human Well-Being: A Framework for Assessment* (Island Press, 2003).

61 Ibid., 3.
62 See Millennium Ecosystem Assessment, www.millenniumassessment.org/en/ Global.html; World Resources Institute, *Ecosystem Services: A Guide for Decisionmakers* (WRI, 2008), http://pdf.wri.org/ecosystem_services_guide_for_ decisionmakers.pdf; EC and UNEP Initiative – 'The Economics of Ecosystems and Biodiversity' (2008), www.teebweb.org.
63 Barnthouse and Stahl, 'Assessing and Managing Natural Resource Damages: Continuing Challenges and Opportunities', op cit, 714.

Conclusion

Introduction

This study has revealed several avenues that merit further consideration in the assessment of compensation for environmental damage. First, courts and tribunals have a margin to consider equitable considerations in their awards for damages. This could be used to take into account the behaviour of the parties, an ecosystems approach and the fight against climate change. Second, courts and tribunals can be appropriate venues to consider complex matters of science, but a more consistent practice on recourse to experts should be developed. Third, the nexus with human rights is likely to become more relevant in assessments of environmental compensation as we become increasingly aware of the impact that environmental damage can have on the rights of individuals or communities. The responsibility of private entities to respect human rights has also become increasingly evident in recent litigation, conventional and other international practice.[1]

In the context of environmental compensation, international and national jurisprudence illustrate that there are many ways of calculating monetary compensation for environmental damage, and their outcomes vary significantly. This is particularly evident in the major discrepancies that can exist between claimant, respondent and tribunal assessments of environmental damage. As such, it is important to clarify the practice on environmental compensation. For example, in the *Costa Rica v. Nicaragua (Compensation)* case, Costa Rica claimed for almost USD7 million in damages, while Nicaragua estimated that Costa Rica was not entitled to anything more than around USD190,000.[2] The Court ultimately awarded almost USD380,000, which represented about 5% of Costa Rica's claim. Similarly, in the *Perenco v. Ecuador* ICSID case, the tribunal complained that the parties were 'effectively shooting at different targets' in their assessments and that this made the tribunal's task very difficult.[3] In light of the vast sums at stake and the wildly different calculations, as well as the critical need for robust environmental protection, it is apparent that coherent guidance on assessing environmental damage in monetary terms is required.

This concluding chapter synthesises the specific aspects of judicial practice that merit development in the area of compensation for environmental damage.

The need for equitable considerations

Equitable considerations have been referred to or encouraged by courts and tribunals, judges, scholars or institutions where broader concerns may be at stake in a given dispute. As noted in Chapter 3, for example, the 1997 resolution of the *Institut de droit international* on 'Responsibility and Liability under International Law for Environmental Damage' refers to equitable assessment in determining amounts of compensation.[4] Similarly, Judge Ad Hoc Dugard in the *Costa Rica v. Nicaragua (Compensation)* case urged the ICJ to take equitable considerations into account in its appraisal of environmental compensation.[5] Human rights courts, as was evident in the European Court of Human Rights case of *López Ostra v. Spain*, have regularly invoked equitable considerations when assessing damages.[6] Indeed, equitable considerations could give latitude to factor into a quantification of damages the protection of the environment, the behaviour of the parties or measures designed to abate climate change, for example, even if punitive or exemplary damages are not permitted under international law.

Indeed, it has been suggested that there may be some margin to take behaviour into account where the conduct of the party who has caused environmental damage has been particularly egregious or deliberate.[7] Such considerations should encompass the degree of fault, the breach of an international rule, the severity of the violation or aggravated damages and any intent or negligence.[8] Indeed, in the arbitral practice of international economic law, the amount of compensation for expropriated property can vary depending on whether the taking was lawful or unlawful.[9] The contributory fault of the claimant may also be factored in, as is relatively well-established under international law in the determination of reparation.[10] There is therefore some precedent for taking into account the conduct of all parties in the assessment of damages in international litigation.

This may be one way that the retributive theory, particularly the idea that the perpetrator owes a debt to society that must be repaid, may be reconciled with the present prevailing view that punitive damages are not permitted under international law.[11] Where environmental damage becomes more costly, there is also likely to be a deterrent effect.[12]

Once again, in the *Costa Rica v. Nicaragua (Compensation)*, dissenting Judge Ad Hoc Dugard was of the view that Nicaragua's behaviour and the gravity of the wrongful act should have been factored into the ICJ's assessment of the compensation it awarded to Costa Rica:

> [i]n assessing compensation in this case, the Court should have had regard to the gravity of Nicaragua's unlawful activities. The amount of compensation should be assessed so as to fit the wrongful conduct. This was made clear by the International Law Commission in its Commentary on the Draft Articles on the Responsibility of States for Internationally Wrongful Acts when it declared:

> > As to the appropriate heads of compensable damage and the principles of assessment to be applied in quantification, these will vary, depending upon the content of particular primary obligations, *an evaluation of the respective behaviour of the parties* and, more generally, a concern to reach *an equitable* and acceptable outcome.[13]

This suggests that, in the gravest cases of misconduct involving the environment, courts and tribunals should and could factor equitable considerations such as the behaviour of parties into an assessment of damages. The law of State responsibility, as observed by Judge Ad Hoc Dugard, in fact encourages the consideration of the behaviour of the parties and equitable considerations in the determination of compensation.

The need for an ecosystem services approach

While an ecosystems approach is not yet a requirement of customary international law, it is increasingly evident in international environmental law.[14] As explored in Chapter 3, an ecosystems approach is becoming more and more prevalent in multilateral environmental agreements and other instruments of international environmental law. This development suggests that courts and tribunals should take account of the wide variety of possible damage and reflect the evolving nature of scientific understanding.

We should not exclude from view damage that cannot be valued by reference to market value or the loss of environmental goods and services that may have no economic value to human beings. A more complex understanding of the environment, by adopting an ecosystem services approach, can help to reveal the values of the environment that would otherwise remain hidden. For example, where an environment is damaged such that its capacity for carbon sequestration is diminished, it would be appropriate to take measures to restore that capacity by taking measures to offset carbon emissions, even while the affected area is being restored to its original state.

Similarly, lost trees may affect the air quality in the area, which can in turn create public health problems and, therefore, increase the overall costs of environmental damage to individuals or society. As such, it may be necessary to ensure that additional measures are taken to maintain air quality levels while the original site is being restored. An ecosystems approach to environmental damage assessment and valuation can ensure that essential services provided by ecosystems do not go unremedied in the short or long term.

We should learn from methods developed beyond international law in this respect. Indeed, various approaches can be detected in selected case law from national jurisdictions concerning the evaluation of environmental damage and the award of compensation. Generally speaking, courts are becoming more amenable to recognising broader notions of damage and compensable values, such as ecological damage or damage to the environment per se.

Interestingly, the US approach provides for compensation for the loss of the use of natural resources as well as non-use value lost while the environment is being repaired. Moreover, under the US legislation, during restoration, an equivalent site should be provided where the original site is significantly damaged. Further still, EU and US regimes provide for interim losses, that is losses incurred while the affected site is being repaired. This is generally not the case in international regimes, but a strong argument can be made that it should be. Indeed, to give one example of why it may be important for international regimes to follow suit, it is now the case that individualised obligations exist for States in respect of gas emissions under the Paris Agreement.[15] States are required to set their own targets on greenhouse gas emissions through so-called nationally determined contributions (NDCs), which are assessed and revised periodically. States who have their environment damaged and carbon sinks diminished in effectiveness, for example through deforestation, may have to take additional measures to mitigate their greenhouse gas emissions and ensure they meet their NDCs.

In evaluating environmental damage, it is important to recognise that significant intangible harm is likely to result from climate change, in addition to tangible economic harm. Indeed, climate-related harm is likely to result from floods, droughts, increased temperature and heat waves, among many other tangible values, but climate-related harm can also affect culture, lifestyle, traditions and heritage, physical health, mental and emotional wellbeing and human mobility, as well as many other intangible values.[16] Broader conceptions of environmental damage should raise awareness of these intangible values affected by climate change, which can be exacerbated by environmental damage such as deforestation, for example.

The need for expertise in determining compensation

International courts and tribunals are increasingly being asked to adjudicate upon complex scientific matters. How courts and tribunals deal with science and employ experts is critical to ensuring the protection of global public goods. As such, the recourse to experts among certain international courts and tribunals in the assessment of environmental damage is welcome. For example, some investment tribunals have shown signs that they are taking scientific matters seriously and have appointed their own experts to analyse scientific matters, as was the case in *Perenco v. Ecuador*. In the latter case, the tribunal recognised the difficulty in evaluating environmental damage and compensation on the basis of expert reports provided by the parties and appointed its own expert. The tribunal also allowed the parties' experts to comment on the reports of the tribunal-appointed expert, bolstering the transparency of the approach adopted by the tribunal.[17]

The importance of expertise was also underlined in the practice of the UNCC, which was explored in Chapter 3. Indeed, the UNCC's F4 Panel in one of its reports observed that

[i]n evaluating the scientific and technical appropriateness of monitoring and assessment activities and assessing the reasonableness of the expenses claimed, the Panel was assisted by expert consultants retained by the Commission. In view of the complexity of the issues and the need to consider scientific, legal, social, commercial and accounting issues in evaluating the claims and assessing the amounts of compensation, the Panel considered it desirable and necessary to have the assistance of a multidisciplinary team of experts.[18]

As noted in Chapter 2, we can detect an evolution in international dispute settlement generally, not least in the case law of the ICJ. In the *Pulp Mills on the River Uruguay* case it was noted that those submitting scientific or technical evidence should appear before the Court as experts rather than as counsel, not least so that they could be subjected to cross-examination.[19] Scientific experts have been resorted to in the *Whaling in the Antarctic* case,[20] as well as in the *Construction of a Road in Costa Rica along the San Juan River* case[21] and in the *Maritime Delimitation in the Caribbean Sea and the Pacific Ocean* case.[22] Beyond the ICJ, in the *South China Sea Arbitration Between the Republic of the Philippines and the People's Republic of China*, the tribunal appointed its own *ex curia* experts so that the tribunal could form its own independent opinion on the environmental impact of the activities conducted by China in the South China Sea.[23]

That said, there remain several legitimacy issues around the use of experts, particularly as regards the distinctions between law and fact, as well as improving certain procedural safeguards, such as cross-examination or that the parties have the possibility to respond to and comment upon expertise provided by tribunal-appointed experts. The design of such safeguards could be inspired by, for example, those provided for under the ICJ or WTO's rules on the involvement of experts in proceedings.[24]

The need to recognise the nexus between environmental damage and human rights

Many resolutions of the UN Human Rights Council have recognised the relationship between a healthy environment and the full realization of human rights.[25] A Special Rapporteur on human rights and the environment was appointed in 2015,[26] and in 2017 the Special Rapporteur warned in his annual report that pollution is one of the main causes of biodiversity degradation which, in turn, hinders the full realization of human rights.[27] Moreover, the Special Rapporteur on toxic dumping has highlighted the profound consequences of toxic dumping, not just for the natural environment and ecosystems but also for human beings and the realisation of their fundamental rights.[28]

The Inter-American Court of Human Rights' Advisory Opinion on *The Environment and Human Rights* is a further example of recognition of the link between the environment and human rights.[29] The Court found that States should take measures to ensure significant environmental harm is not caused to individuals within or beyond their territory.[30] In establishing a justiciable right to a healthy environment under the American Convention on Human Rights, this Opinion suggests those in third countries may bring a case where their rights have been impaired by environmental damage. This is, once again, especially relevant in the context of growing climate litigation.

Moreover, given the interconnected nature of the environment and the likely widespread effects of environmental damage, it may be appropriate to consider environmental compensation for third parties whose rights have been violated by the effects of an incident far away. For example, where environmental damage exacerbates climate change or the water cycle is affected by pollution, the reach of damage may extend far away from the site of the incident.

Concluding remarks

When appraising environmental damage and awarding compensation, courts and tribunals should be mindful of the full extent that damage can cause. In particular, the impact of environmental damage on the climate and on human rights should be taken into account. Scientific understanding has evolved at a fast pace in recent years, and areas of international environmental law are similarly starting to reflect this new understanding. International courts and tribunals have previously opined on the need to be cognisant of new norms, principles and standards of international environmental law.[31] Indeed, primary obligations of full, fair or adequate compensation should be read in light of the contemporary landscape of international environmental law as well as new scientific understanding.

Generally speaking, international courts and tribunals have shown that they are increasingly amenable to environmental concerns. This is evident not least in certain approaches to scientific matters, recourse to experts and their finding that environmental impact assessments are required under customary international law, for example. Indeed, the recent international cases considered in this study evidence a trend towards the environment becoming a more regular feature of international adjudication.[32] Despite their occasional flaws, the statements of principle made by various courts and tribunals in cases involving environmental damage and compensation likely lay a firmer foundation for the litigation of environmental matters in the future. We should also recall previous developments in the practice of the UNCC or other international regimes, as well as at the domestic and regional levels. Further still, economics and philosophy have developed various methods and concepts that take broader considerations into account in valuing environmental damage. In the present hostile climate around matters of the environment in the political arena, these all give hope that 'oaks may still grow strong in contrary winds'.[33]

Notes

1 See, for example *Urbaser SA and Consorcio de Aguas Bilbao Bizkaia, Bilbao Biskaia Ur Partzuergoa v. The Argentine Republic*, Award, ICSID Case No. ARB/07/26 (8 December 2016); *Bear Creek Mining v. Peru*, Award, ICSID Case No. ARB/14/21 (30 November 2017); Draft Hague Rules on Business and Human Rights Arbitration, www.cilc.nl/cms/wp-content/uploads/2019/06/Draft-BHR-Rules-Final-version-for-Public-consultation.pdf; Jason Rudall, 'Recent Interactions between Investment Protection, Environmental Concerns and Human Rights: New Emulsion or Still Immiscible?', *Blog: International Law @ UEA*, www.uea.ac.uk/law/research/international-law-blog.
2 *Certain Activities Carried Out By Nicaragua in the Border Area (Costa Rica v. Nicaragua) (Compensation)*, ICJ General List No. 150 (2 February 2018).
3 *Perenco v. Ecuador and Empresa Estatal Petróleos del Ecuador (Petroecuador)*, ICSID Case No. ARB/08/6, Interim Decision on the Environmental Counterclaim (11 August 2015), para 581.
4 Institut de droit international, *Responsibility and Liability under International Law for Environmental Damage* (Strasbourg, 1997).

5 *Costa Rica v. Nicaragua (Compensation)*, Dissenting Opinion: Judge *Ad Hoc* Dugard, 8.
6 *López Ostra v. Spain*, Application No. 16798/90, A/303-C [1995] 20 EHRR 277.
7 Francisco Orrego Vicuña, 'Responsibility and Liability for Environmental Damage Under International Law: Issues and Trends' 10 (1998) *Georgetown International Environmental Law Review* 292.
8 Louise de La Fayette, 'The Concept of Environmental Damage in International Liability Regimes' in Michael Bowman and Alan Boyle (eds.), *Environmental Damage in International and Comparative Law: Problems of Definition and Valuation* (Oxford University Press, 2002), 186.
9 See, for example, *Libyan American Oil Company (LIAMCO) v. Government of Libya* [1982] 62 ILR 141, 202; *Government of Kuwait v. American Independent Oil Company (Aminoil)* [1982] 66 ILR 529, 600; *Amoco International Finance Corporation v. The Government of the Islamic Republic of Iran* [1987] 15 I Iran-U.S.C.T.R. 189, 246.
10 See, for example, *The 'Wimbledon' (Government of His Britannic Majesty et al v. German Empire)* [1923] PCIJ Series A, No. 1, 32; *LaGrand (Germany v. United States)* [2001] ICJ Rep 466; Article 39, Draft Articles on the Responsibility of States for Internationally Wrongful Acts II(2) YBILC (2001).
11 F. Comte, 'Environmental Crime and the Police in Europe: A Panorama and Possible Paths for Future Action' 15(7) (2006) *European Environmental Law Review* 190, 196.
12 Michael Faure and Göran Skogh, *The Economic Analysis of Environmental Policy and Law* (Edward Elgar, 2003), 287.
13 *Costa Rica v. Nicaragua (Compensation)*, Dissenting Opinion of Judge Ad Hoc Dugard.
14 See Owen McIntyre, 'Protection and Preservation of Freshwater Ecosystems (Articles 20–23)' in Laurence Boisson de Chazournes, Makane Moïse Mbengue, Mara Tignino, Komlan Sangbana, and Jason Rudall (eds.), *The UN Convention on the Law of the Non-Navigational Uses of International Watercourses: A Commentary* (Oxford University Press, 2018); see also Owen McIntyre, 'The Role of Customary Rules and Principles in the Environmental Protection of Shared International Freshwater Resources' 46(1) (2006) *Natural Resources Journal* 157.
15 Article 4, Paris Agreement under the United Nations Framework Convention on Climate Change, 22 April 2016, entry into force 4 November 2016.
16 Petra Tschakert, Neville Ellis, Christopher Anderson, A. Kelly and James Obeng, 'One Thousand Ways to Experience Loss: A Systematic Analysis of Climate-Related Intangible Harm from Around the World' 55 (2019) *Global Environmental Change* 58, 62.
17 *Perenco v. Ecuador*, para 588.
18 UNCC, *Report and Recommendations Made By the Panel of Commissioners Concerning the First Instalment of 'F4' Claims* (22 June 2001), UN Doc. S/AC.26/2001/16, para 42.
19 *Pulp Mills on the River Uruguay (Argentina v. Uruguay)* [2001] ICJ Rep 14, para 167.
20 *Whaling in the Antarctic (Australia v. Japan)* [2014] ICJ Rep 226, paras 74–5.
21 *Construction of a Road in Costa Rica along the San Juan River (Nicaragua v. Costa Rica)*, Judgment (16 December 2015), paras 45, 175–6, 204.
22 *Maritime Delimitation in the Caribbean Sea and the Pacific Ocean (Costa Rica v. Nicaragua) / Land Boundary in the Northern Part of Isla Portillos (Costa Rica v. Nicaragua)*, General List Nos. 157 and 165 (2 February 2018), paras 14, 71, 73, and 86.

23 *South China Sea Arbitration between the Republic of the Philippines and the People's Republic of China*, Award, PCA Case No. 2013–19, paras 84, 136 and 821.

24 See Makane Moïse Mbengue, 'The Role of Experts before the International Court of Justice: The Whaling in the Antarctic Case' (2015) *Questions of International Law, Zoom-in* 14, 3–12.

25 See, for example, HRC Resolution 16/11 of 24 March 2011 on human rights and the environment; HRC Resolutions 7/23 of 28 March 2008, 10/4 of 25 March 2009 and 18/22 of 30 September 2011 on human rights and climate change; HRC Resolutions 9/1 of 24 September 2008 and 12/18 of 2 October 2009 on the adverse effects of the movement and dumping of toxic and dangerous products and wastes on the enjoyment of human rights; and HRC Resolution 18/11 of 29 September 2011 on the mandate of the Special Rapporteur on the implications for human rights of the environmentally sound management and disposal of hazardous substances and wastes.

26 HRC Resolution 28/11 of 26 March 2015 on human rights and the environment.

27 Report of the Special Rapporteur on the issue of human rights obligations relating to the enjoyment of a safe, clean, healthy and sustainable environment, Biodiversity, UN Doc. A/HRC/34/49, 3.

28 See also, Commission on Human Rights, Special Rapporteur to the UN Commission on Human Rights, *Adverse Effects of the Illicit Movement and Dumping of Toxic and Dangerous Products and Wastes on the Enjoyment of Human Rights* (21 December 2000), UN Doc. E/CN.4/2001/55/Add.1, para 58.

29 *The Environment and Human Rights (State Obligations in Relation to the Environment in the Context of the Protection and Guarantee of the Rights to Life and to Personal Integrity: Interpretation and Scope of Articles 4(1) and 5(1) of the American Convention on Human Rights)*, Advisory Opinion OC-23/17, Inter-Am Ct HR Series A, No. 23.

30 Ibid.

31 *Case Concerning the Gabčikovo-Nagymaros Project (Hungary/Slovakia)* [1997] ICJ Rep 7, 78; *Indus Waters Kishenganga Arbitration (Pakistan v. India)*, Partial Award, PCA Case No. 2011–01, para 111.

32 See, for example, *Burlington Resources v. Ecuador*, op cit; *Perenco v. Ecuador*, op cit; *The Environment and Human Rights (State Obligations in Relation to the Environment in the Context of the Protection and Guarantee of the Rights to Life and to Personal Integrity: Interpretation and Scope of Articles 4(1) and 5(1) of the American Convention on Human Rights)*, op cit; *Dispute Concerning Delimitation of the Maritime Boundary between Ghana and Cote d'Ivoire in the Atlantic Ocean (Ghana/Cote d'Ivoire)*, ITLOS Case No. 23 (23 September 2017). For a fuller exploration of trends and prospects in the extension of environmental protection through litigation, see Jason Rudall, *Altruism in International Law* (Cambridge University Press, forthcoming).

33 An adaptation of the Peter Marshall quotation: 'When We Long for Life without Difficulty, Remind Us That Oaks Grow Strong under Contrary Winds and Diamonds Are Made under Pressure', www.goodreads.com/author/quotes/33254. Peter_Marshall.

Bibliography

Books

Alder, J., and Wilkinson, D. *Environmental Law and Ethics* (Springer, 1999).

Attfield, R. *The Ethics of Environmental Concern* (2nd ed., University of Georgia Press, 1991).

Boisson de Chazournes, L. *Fresh Water in International Law* (Oxford University Press, 2013).

Faure, M., and Skogh, G. *The Economic Analysis of Environmental Policy and Law* (Edward Elgar, 2003).

Grotius, H. *De Jure Belli Ac Pacis* [1625], Liber secundus, caput XVII (Nijhoff, 1948).

Hanley, N., Shogren, J., and White, B. *An Introduction to Environmental Economics* (Oxford University Press, 2001).

Hardman Reis, T. *Compensation for Environmental Damages under International Law* (Wolters Kluwer, 2011).

Hausman, J. *Contingent Valuation: A Critical Assessment* (Emerald Publishing, 1993).

Mathews, F. *The Ecological Self* (Routledge, 1991).

Pufendorf, P. *Elementorum Jurisprudentiae Universalis – Libri Duo* 1672 (University of Lausanne, 2010).

Quintana, J. *Litigation at the International Court of Justice: Practice and Procedure* (Brill, 2015).

Rolston, H. *Conserving Natural Value* (Columbia University Press, 1994).

Rudall, J. *Altruism in International Law* (Cambridge University Press, forthcoming).

Shelton, D. *Remedies in International Human Rights Law* (Oxford University Press, 1999).

Vanderheiden, S. *Atmospheric Justice: A Political Theory of Climate Change* (Oxford University Press, 2009).

Wewerinke-Singh, M. *State Responsibility, Climate Change and Human Rights under International Law* (Hart, 2019).

Wolff, C. *Jus Gentium Methodo Scientica Pertractatum* 1764 (Clarendon Press, 1934).

Wolff, C. *Principes du droit de la nature et des gens* 1758 (Presses Universitaires de Caen, 2011).

Yang, T., Telesetsky, A., Harmon-Walker, L., and Percival, R. *Comparative and Global Environmental Law and Policy* (Wolters Kluwer, 2019).

Chapters and articles

Barnthouse, L., and Stahl, R. 'Assessing and Managing Natural Resource Damages: Continuing Challenges and Opportunities' 59 (2017) *Environmental Management* 709.

Bateman, I., Langford, I., and Rasbash, J. 'Willingness-to-Pay Question Format Effects in Contingent Valuation Studies' in Ian Bateman and Ken Willis (eds.), *Valuation of Environmental Preferences: Theory and Practice of the Contingent Valuation Method in the US, EU and Developing Countries* (Oxford University Press, 2001).

Bianchi, A. 'Harm to the Environment in Italian Practice: The Interaction of International Law and Domestic Law' in Peter Wetterstein (ed.), *Harm to the Environment: The Right to Compensation and the Assessment of Damages* (Clarendon Press, 1997).

Boisson de Chazournes, L., and Campanelli, D. 'The United Nations Compensation Commission: Time for an Assessment?' in Andreas Fischer-Lescano et al. (eds.), *Frieden in Freiheit = Peace in liberty = Paix en liberté: Festschrift für Michael Bothe zum 70 Geburtstag* (Nomos, 2008).

Boisson de Chazournes, L., Mbengue, M., Das, R., and Gros, G. 'One Size Does Not Fit All: Uses of Experts before International Courts and Tribunals: An Insight Into the Practice' 9(3) (2018) *Journal of International Dispute Settlement* 477.

Bowman, M. 'Biodiversity, Intrinsic Value, and the Definition and Valuation of Environmental Harm' in Michael Bowman and Alan Boyle (eds.), *Environmental Damage in International and Comparative Law: Problems of Definition and Valuation* (Oxford University Press, 2002).

Boyle, A. 'Reparation for Environmental Damage in International Law: Some Preliminary Problems' in Michael Bowman and Alan Boyle (eds.), *Environmental Damage in International and Comparative Law: Problems of Definition and Valuation* (Oxford University Press, 2002).

Brunnée, J., and Toope, S. 'Environmental Security and Freshwater Resources: A Case for International Ecosystem Law' 5 (1994) *Yearbook of International Environmental Law* 41.

Burkett, M. 'A Justice Paradox: Climate Change, Small Island Developing States, and the Absence of International Legal Remedy' in Carmen Gonzales and Sumudu Atapattu (eds.), *International Environmental Law and the Global South* (Cambridge University Press, 2015).

Comte, F. 'Environmental Crime and the Police in Europe: A Panorama and Possible Paths for Future Action' 15(7) (2006) *European Environmental Law Review* 190.

de Brabandere, E. 'Human Rights and Foreign Direct Investment' in Markus Krajewski and Rhea Hoffmann (eds.), *Research Handbook on Foreign Direct Investment* (Edward Elgar, 2018).

de La Fayette, L. 'The Concept of Environmental Damage in International Liability Regimes' in Michael Bowman and Alan Boyle (eds.), *Environmental Damage in International and Comparative Law: Problems of Definition and Valuation* (Oxford University Press, 2002).

Desvousges, W., Gard, N., Michael, H., and Chance, A. 'Habitat and Resource Equivalency Analysis: A Critical Assessment' 143 (2018) *Ecological Economics* 74.

de Visscher, C. 'La Contribution de l'Institut de Droit International au développement du droit international' in *Institut de Droit International, Livre du Centenaire 1873–1973: Evolution et Perspectives du Droit International* 128 (Karger, 1973).

de Vitoria, F. 'Second Relectio: On the Indians [1538–1539]' in J. Brown Scott (ed.), *The Spanish Origins of International Law: Francisco de Vitoria and His Law of Nations* (Clarendon Press, 1934).

Diamond, P., and Hausman, J. 'Contingent Valuation: Is Some Number Better Than No Number?' *Journal of Economic Perspectives* 45.

Farber, D. 'The UNCC as a Model for Climate Compensation' in Cymie R. Payne and Peter H. Sand (eds.), *Gulf War Reparations and the UN Compensation Commission* (Oxford University Press, 2011).

Farber, S. 'Undesirable Facilities and Property Values: A Summary of Empirical Studies' 24(1) (1998) *Ecological Economics* 1.

Feria-Tinta, M., and Milnes, S. 'The Rise of Environmental Law in International Dispute Resolution: Inter-American Court of Human Rights Issues Advisory Opinion on Environment and Human Rights' 27 (2016) *Yearbook of International Environmental Law* 64.

Flint, M. 'Biological Diversity and Developing Countries' in Anil Markandya and Julie Richardson (eds.), *Earthscan Reader in Environmental Economics* (Taylor and Francis, 1992).

Foster, V., Bateman, I., and Harley, D. 'Real versus Hypothetical Willingness to Pay for Environmental Protection' 48(2) (1997) *Journal of Agricultural Economics* 123.

Francis, G. 'Ecosystem Management' 33 (1993) *Natural Resources Journal* 315.

Frikblom, P. 'Hypothetical Question Modes and Real Willingness to Pay' 34(3) (1997) *Journal of Environmental Economics and Management* 275.

Garrod, G., and Willis, K. 'The Amenity Value of Woodland in Great Britain' 2(4) (1992) *Environmental and Resource Economics* 415.

Hambro, E. 'The Centenary of the Institut de Droit International' 43 (1973) *Nordisk Tidsskrift for International Ret* 9.

Hanley, N. 'The Economic Value of Environmental Damage' in Michael Bowman and Alan Boyle (eds.), *Environmental Damage in International and Comparative Law: Problems of Definition and Valuation* (Oxford University Press, 2002).

Huguenin, M., Donlan, M., van Geel, A., and Paterson, R. 'Assessment and Valuation of Damage to the Environment' in Cymie Payne and Peter Sand (eds.), *Gulf War Reparations and the UN Compensation Commission* (Oxford University Press, 2011).

Kahneman, D., and Tversky, A. 'Prospect Theory: An Analysis of Decision under Risk' 47(4) (1979) *Econometrica* 263.

Kazazi, M. 'An Overview of Evidence before the United Nations Compensation Commission' 1 (1999) *International Law Forum* 219.

Mbengue, M. 'The Role of Experts before the International Court of Justice: The Whaling in the Antarctic Case' (2015) *Questions of International Law, Zoom-in* 14.

McIntyre, O. 'Protection and Preservation of Freshwater Ecosystems (Articles 20–23)' in Laurence Boisson de Chazournes, Makane Moïse Mbengue, Mara Tignino, Komlan Sangbana and Jason Rudall (eds.), *The UN Convention on the Law of the Non-Navigational Uses of International Watercourses: A Commentary* (Oxford University Press, 2018).

McIntyre, O. 'The Role of Customary Rules and Principles in the Environmental Protection of Shared International Freshwater Resources' 46(1) (2006) *Natural Resources Journal* 157.

Munro, A., and Hanley, N. 'Information, Uncertainty and Contingent Valuation' in Ian Bateman and Ken Willis (eds.), *Valuation of Environmental Preferences: Theory and Practice of the Contingent Valuation Method in the US, EU and Developing Countries* (Oxford University Press, 2001).

Payne, C. 'Developments in the Law of Environmental Reparations: A Case Study of the UN Compensation Commission' in Carsten Stahn, Jens Iverson and Jennifer Easterday (eds.), *Environmental Protection and Transitions from Conflict to Peace: Clarifying Norms, Principles and Practices* (Oxford University Press, 2017).

Pearce, D., and Moran, D. 'The Economics of Biological Diversity Conservation' in Peggy Fiedler and Peter Kareiva (eds.), *Conservation Biology: For the Coming Decade* (Chapman and Hall, 1998).

Portney, P. 'The Contingent Valuation Debate: Why Economists Should Care' 8(4) (1994) *Journal of Economic Perspectives* 3.

Preston, B. 'Characteristics of Successful Environmental Courts and Tribunals' 26 (2014) *Journal of Environmental Law* 365.

Rudall, J. 'Certain Activities Carried Out by Nicaragua in the Border Area (Costa Rica v. Nicaragua): Compensation Owed by the Republic of Nicaragua to the Republic of Costa Rica' 112(2) (2018) *American Journal of International Law* 288.

Rudall, J. 'The Interplay between the UN Watercourses Convention and International Environmental Law' in Laurence Boisson de Chazournes, Makane Moïse Mbengue, Mara Tignino, Komlan Sangbana and Jason Rudall (eds.), *The UN Convention on the Law of the Non-Navigational Uses of International Watercourses: A Commentary* (Oxford University Press, 2018).

Rudall, J. 'Not Just a Wit, But a Cause of Wit in Others: The Influence of Human Rights in International Litigation' in Avidan Kent, Nikos Skoutaris and Jamie Trinidad (eds.), *The Future of International Courts: Regional, Institutional and Procedural Challenges* (Routledge, 2019).

Sand, P. 'Compensation for Environmental Damage from the 1991 Gulf War' 35 (2005) *Environmental Policy and Law* 244.

Sand, P. 'Environmental Dispute Settlement and the Experience of the UN Compensation Committee' 54 (2011) *Japanese Yearbook of International Law* 151.

Sand, P. 'Environmental Principles Applied' in Cymie Payne and Peter Sand (eds.), *Gulf War Reparations and the UN Compensation Commission* (Oxford University Press, 2011).

Schwermer, S. *Economic Valuation of Environmental Damage: Methodological Convention 2.0 for Estimates of Environmental Costs* (Umwelt Bundesamt, 2012).

Teclaff, L., and Teclaff, E. 'International Control of Cross-Media Pollution: An Ecosystem Approach' 27 (1987) *Natural Resources Journal* 21.

Teitel, R., and Howse, R. 'Cross-Judging: Tribunalization in a Fragmented but Interconnected Global Order' 41(1) (2008) *New York University Journal of International Law and Politics* 959.

Tschakert, P., Ellis, N., Anderson, C., Kelly, A., and Obeng, J. 'One Thousand Ways to Experience Loss: A Systematic Analysis of Climate-Related Intangible Harm from Around the World' 55 (2019) *Global Environmental Change* 58.

Unworth, R., and Bishop, R. 'Assessing Natural Resource Damages Using Environmental Annuities' 11 (1994) *Ecological Economics* 35.

Vicuña, F. 'Responsibility and Liability for Environmental Damage under International Law: Issues and Trends' 10 (1998) *Georgetown International Environmental Law Review* 292.

Vöneky, S. 'The Liability Annex to the Protocol on Environmental Protection to the Antarctic Treaty' in Doris König, Peter-Tobias Stoll, Volker Röben and Nele Matz-Lück (eds.), *International Law Today: New Challenges and the Need for Reform?* (Springer, 2007).

Wetterstein, P. 'Environmental Damage in the Legal Systems of the Nordic Countries and Germany' in Michael Bowman and Alan Boyle (eds.), *Environmental Damage in International and Comparative Law* (Oxford University Press, 2002).

Wetterstein, P. 'A Proprietary or Possessory Interest: A Conditio Sine Qua Non for Claiming Damages for Environmental Impairment?' in Peter Wetterstein (ed.), *Harm to the Environment: The Right to Compensation and the Assessment of Damages* (Clarendon Press, 1997).

Online resources

Bousso, R. 'BP Deepwater Horizon Costs Balloon to $65 Billion', *Reuters*, 16 January 2018, www.reuters.com/article/us-bp-deepwaterhorizon/bp-deepwater-horizon-costs-balloon-to-65-billion-idUSKBN1F50NL

Desierto, D. 'Why Arbitrate Business and Human Rights Disputes? Public Consultation Period Open for the Draft Hague Rules on Business and Human Rights Arbitration', *EJIL: Talk!*, 12 July 2019.

International Oil Pollution Compensation Funds (IOPC), 'Compensation', https://iopcfunds.org/compensation/

International Oil Pollution Compensation Funds (IOPC), 'Incidents', www.iopcfunds.org/incidents/incident-map/

Marsili, A. 'A New Court in Guatemala Tackles Ecoside', *FrontLines*, 2015, www.usaid.gov/news-information/frontlines/resilience-2015/new-court-guatemala-tackles-ecocide

Millennium Ecosystem Assessment, www.millenniumassessment.org/en/Global.html
National Oceanic and Atmospheric Administration, 'Deepwater Horizon Oil Spill Settlements: Where the Money Went', www.noaa.gov/explainers/deepwater-horizon-oil-spill-settlements-where-money-went
'Resource Equivalency Methods for Assessing Environmental Damage in the EU (REMEDE) Toolkit', www.envliability.eu
Rudall, J. 'Recent Interactions between Investment Protection, Environmental Concerns and Human Rights: New Emulsion or Still Immiscible?', *Blog: International Law @ UEA*, www.uea.ac.uk/law/research/international-law-blog
UNCC, https://uncc.ch/home
UN Environment Programme, 'The Economics of Ecosystems and Biodiversity' (2008), www.teebweb.org
United Nations Compensation Commission (UNCC), 'Follow-up Programme for Environmental Awards', https://uncc.ch/follow-programme-environmental-awards-0
World Resources Institute, 'Ecosystem Services: A Guide for Decisionmakers', *WRI*, 2008, http://pdf.wri.org/ecosystem_services_guide_for_decisionmakers.pdf

Index

Note: Page numbers followed by 'n' refer to notes.

For Product Safety Concerns and Information please contact our EU
representative GPSR@taylorandfrancis.com
Taylor & Francis Verlag GmbH, Kaufingerstraße 24, 80331 München, Germany

www.ingramcontent.com/pod-product-compliance
Lightning Source LLC
Chambersburg PA
CBHW050533270326
41926CB00015B/3204